HOW TO PASS

SELECTION TESTS

*We dedicate this book to Nima Modha-Bhatti
and Ella Schlesinger*

HOW TO PASS

SELECTION TESTS

3RD EDITION

Mike Bryon & Sanjay Modha

KOGAN
PAGE

Publisher's note

Every possible effort has been made to ensure that the information contained in this book is accurate at the time of going to press, and the publishers and authors cannot accept responsibility for any errors or omissions, however caused. No responsibility for loss or damage occasioned to any person acting, or refraining from action, as a result of the material in this publication can be accepted by the editor, the publisher or any of the authors.

First published in 1991
Revised edition 1992
Reprinted 1994. Title changed to *How to Pass Selection Tests*
Reprinted 1995, 1996, 1997
Second edition 1998
Reprinted 1999, 2000
Third edition 2005

120 Pentonville Road   22883 Quicksilver Drive
London N1 9JN   Sterling VA 20166–2012
United Kingdom   USA
www.kogan-page.co.uk

© Mike Bryon and Sanjay Modha 1991, 1998, 2005

The right of Mike Bryon and Sanjay Modha to be identified as the authors of this work has been asserted by them in accordance with the Copyright, Designs and Patents Act 1988.

British Library Cataloguing-in-Publication Data

A CIP record for this book is available from the British Library.

ISBN 0 7494 4374 X

Library of Congress Cataloging-in-Publication Data

Bryon, Mike.
    How to pass selection tests / Mike Bryon and Sanjay Modha.—3rd ed.
        p. cm.
    ISBN 0-7494-4374-X
    1. Employment tests.   I. Modha, Sanjay. II. Title.
HF5549.5.E5B78 2005
658.3'1125—dc22

                                2005009397

Typeset by Saxon Graphics Ltd, Derby
Printed and bound in Great Britain by Creative Print and Design (Wales), Ebbw Vale

Contents

Introduction

In recent years there has been a huge increase in the use of selection tests. The increase has been particularly pronounced in the area of employment with many more employers now relying on a test to help them decide between candidates.

As well as becoming far more popular, the style and method of testing has also changed. In a test today the questions are more likely to describe work situations, and their relevance to the job will be much more obvious. Far more common are questions about your personality and preferred working style. A test these days may well be taken at a computer terminal although tests administrated with paper and pen are still very common.

Tests have changed over recent years but you still need to be well prepared to succeed. Lots of practice is essential if you are to show your full potential in a selection or psychometric test and this is why this book is so valuable. It contains many hundreds of really relevant questions that will allow you to prepare for the most common tests in use today. If you are applying for work in an office environment, in business, finance, administration or media then you will find it essential preparation.

The Kogan Page testing series includes titles aimed at all levels and most areas of testing. This book is the ideal starting point for a candidate facing tests at the intermediate level. Recommended sources of further practice are also provided.

The idea for this book arose from our work in pre-employment training for some of the largest employers in the UK. Our work involved preparing people for the selection process of these organisations and the posts that they would go on to fill. This experience led us to conclude that many people who fail the tests could in fact pass them. What is required is that they come to terms with their anxieties and prepare well prior to the test.

The purpose of this book is to make available to a general readership the strategies developed while preparing candidates for the selection tests.

Since its publication in 1991, *How to Pass Selection Tests* has become a best-seller and proved of considerable help to thousands of people who face employers' tests. This third edition ensures that the exercises continue to help candidates prepare for the challenge of selection tests.

Motivated candidates complain that they are unable to obtain sufficient practice material. In response to this we have added over 200 new practice questions and added explanations to some of the answers. You will find material relevant to the majority of tests in use today and by working through the book you will revise essential skills and competencies.

Together with the editors we have tried to ensure that there are no errors in this book. If you find one then please accept our apologies and be kind enough to inform us of it so that it can be removed from the next imprint.

If you are finding it difficult to locate practice questions relevant to the test you face then feel free to contact us through Kogan Page and if we know of a source then we will be happy to provide you with details.

Aims of the book

Many companies and organisations use tests for selection purposes and for many people these tests represent a significant obstacle to obtaining the job or career of their choice. The aim of this book is to inform readers about these tests and provide exercises so that they can practise before sitting a test. Over half the book comprises exercises that are relevant to some of the most common types of selection test currently in use.

Practice can result in significant improvements in performance in most sorts of test. It also boosts confidence and helps individuals to cope with nervousness. It makes individuals less prone to mistakes and ensures that the test is approached proficiently.

Information is provided about the history and nature of tests, and explanations are offered about why companies use tests and what they believe can be concluded from the results. Advice is also given about what to do if you fail.

General information about tests

History of tests

The first standardised test of ability was produced in France at the beginning of the century by Binet. Initially, the tests were developed for use with children for diagnostic purposes. It was not until World War I that testing for adults really began. These tests proved to be valuable in selecting and allocating recruits for different types of work in the armed forces and also for identifying potential officers. During World War II further advances in selection methods were made. Once again, the tests proved to be valuable in allocating different people to a variety of jobs or trades at different levels or grades.

There were certain advantages in using paper and pencil tests in groups (these are also applicable today in industry and commerce). First, it allowed a large number of people to be tested in one sitting. Second, it allowed people to be tested under the same types of conditions, ie, the physical conditions and instructions could be standardised. Third, people could be allocated to jobs or trades for which they had the aptitude rather than simply being rejected or allocated to jobs on the basis of a simple interview – which can be very subjective.

The use of tests in the two wars played an important part in classifying large numbers of people. Since then tests have been developed and adapted for the needs of industry and commerce. Many organisations, particularly the larger ones, now regularly use selection tests because of the advantages referred to above and other advantages to which we shall refer in a later section (see page 22).

What are selection tests?

Selection tests, as the name suggests, are tests that are designed and used for the purpose of selecting and allocating people. The tests can be used in a number of situations; for example, in selecting people for jobs, in promoting or transferring people to other departments or jobs, and in certain types of course. They are also used in redundancy and career counselling and are known as psychometric or psychological tests.

Psychometric tests are one way of establishing or confirming an applicant's competence for the job. They can be useful provided they are reliable and valid for the job for which they are being used. Selection tests are standardised sets of questions or problems that allow an applicant's performance to be compared with that of other people of a similar background. For example, if you happen to be a graduate your score would be compared to those of other graduates, or if you have few or no qualifications your score would be compared to people who are similar to you, and so on. What this means is that the tests are norm referenced (the section dealing with results explains what this means – see page 13).

Reliability and validity

We said that tests can be useful if they are reliable and valid. So what do these two words mean in this context? It is said that a test is *reliable* when consistent results are obtainable. For example, tests that contain ambiguous questions are likely to be unreliable because different people will interpret the questions differently, or even the same person may interpret them differently on different occasions.

Tests are said to be *valid* when they measure what you want them to measure. In personnel selection terms it means that a test must be related in some way to the known demands of the job if it is to be of any use. For example, it needs to be shown that a test score predicts success or failure in a given job.

Figure 2.1 illustrates the kind of relationship that ought to exist between test scores and job performance in which the higher the test score the better the performance in the job. In reality, however, it would be almost impossible to find such a high positive correlation. This is because of the difficulties in measuring job performance in many, if not most, types of job.

Different types of test

In this section we shall look at the various types of psychometric tests and questionnaires that are used. These are attainment and aptitude tests (work sample and trainability tests are also aptitude tests) and personality and interest inventories.

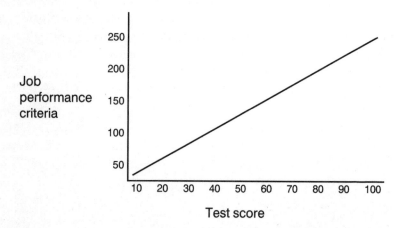

Figure 2.1   *A positive correlation between test scores and job performance*

Ability tests

Ability is the most common aspect of a candidate that is subject to testing, either in the form of paper and pencil tests or some practical exercise. These practical tests are sometimes referred to as performance tests or work sample tests; another variation of these are the trainability tests. We shall deal with these later (see page 8).

Ability tests fall into two main categories: attainment tests and aptitude tests. Aptitude is having either a talent for a particular skill or the potential to acquire it. Attainment is the candidate's current skills and knowledge. It needs to be pointed out that the distinction between attainment tests and aptitude tests is not clear-cut. This is because a single test can be used to measure either attainment or aptitude.

Attainment tests

Attainment tests are those that seek to assess how much skill and knowledge an individual has. For example, an arithmetic test for supermarket cashiers measures attainment as long as it is used to measure arithmetic and not to measure performance as a cashier.

From an employer's point of view an attainment test may provide a better assessment than simply looking at a past record of achievements or non-achievements as the case may be. A standardised test of arithmetic or spelling may give a more reliable indication of relevant present ability than a comparison of school qualifications in maths or English.

From a candidate's point of view an attainment test score will say more to an employer than simply talking about his or her skills. This is particularly useful when the candidate does not possess many, or even any, qualifications.

Aptitude tests

Aptitude tests are used to predict the potential of an individual for a particular job or a course of study. However, as mentioned above, it is not easy to separate tests of potential from tests of attainment because all forms of test assess the person's current skills and knowledge. But the results of that assessment may then be used in a variety of ways. For example:

- to highlight the individual's strengths and weaknesses;
- to provide career counselling;
- to predict success in a job or course.

Work sample tests

Work sample tests are no different from the paper and pencil aptitude tests except that they are practical. They are a miniature version of the job in question. The tasks encompass the main or major elements of a job. They are called work sample tests because that is the main purpose, hence they are sometimes referred to as performance tests.

Trainability tests

Another variation of the work sample test is the trainability test. Trainability testing is a method of assessing applicants' potential for learning new skills in a particular area by carrying out a practical exercise.

Personality questionnaires (tests)

Many people refer to personality inventories or questionnaires as tests. This, however, is misleading because to talk about personality questionnaires as tests implies that there is a pass or fail score, which is not the case.

Personality is something that everyone talks about. You often hear people talking about someone having a 'great personality', but what exactly is it?

There is no one theory or definition of personality with which all psychologists agree, but most personality questionnaires aim to identify certain stable characteristics. They are based on the assumption that the responses to be given will be a representative sample of how an individual will respond in a given social situation, particularly the one in which the selector is interested, ie, the organisation or department in which that individual may be working.

The main characteristics that personality questionnaires aim to identify in an individual are:

Extroversion	Introversion
Tough minded	Tender minded
Independent	Dependent
High self-confidence	Low self-confidence

Interest inventories (tests)

Strictly speaking, interest tests like personality tests are not tests at all, because they are not about obtaining a good or a bad score, or about passing or failing. It is for this reason that they are usually referred to as interest inventories or interest questionnaires. The aim of these interest inventories is to find out an individual's interest in particular occupations.

Interest inventories cover interests in activities such as:

Scientific/technical	– how and why things work or happen
Social/welfare	– helping or caring for people
Persuasion	– influencing people and/or ideas or selling goods and services
Arts	– designing or creating things or ideas
Clerical/computing	– handling data, systems

The use of interest inventories is limited compared to, say, aptitude tests in the selection of applicants. This is because the inventories appear, at least on the face of it, easy to fake. For example, if a person is applying for a position as a clerk, he or she may deliberately indicate a stronger interest in tasks related to the office environment. The interest inventories are probably most useful in vocational guidance where one assumes that people are less likely to fake them.

Fair and unfair discrimination

All good tests discriminate! That, after all, is the purpose of the test. However, this discrimination should be on the basis of ability, and is therefore fair and legal discrimination. If the tests, or the way in which they are used, discriminate on the basis of sex or race it would be unfair and possibly even illegal under the Sex Discrimination Act 1975 and the Race Relations Act 1976.

It does not matter whether the unfair discrimination is intentional or unintentional. However, the Acts do not explicitly refer to testing. The implication of the two Acts is that if the use of the tests (or other selection methods) results in proportionately more women or members of the ethnic minority communities 'failing' the test and as a result not being taken on and the use of the test cannot be justified, this may be unfair discrimination. The onus of proof is on the employer to justify the use of the test.

For example, if an employer sets a condition (let us say a test score of X or above) and a larger proportion of women or ethnic minority groups fail to meet this condition, compared with men or the ethnic majority group, the employer may be required to show that this condition is necessary. If the use of the test can be shown to be justified, the result would be fair discrimination.

When an employer uses tests to select employees, it is on the understanding that the test will differentiate between those candidates with and those without the appropriate skills, knowledge and potential. A test that does not differentiate between the level of abilities in candidates is of no real value to the employer. It is important to the employer that the right person is chosen for the right job. It is equally important to the candidate that it is the right job for him or her. Otherwise the candidate may not be happy in the job or, even worse, he or she may not be capable of doing the job, which can be very demoralising.

Fair discrimination is about distinguishing between people, based on their abilities and aptitudes. These must be shown to be related to the job for which the tests are being used. What this means in practice is that if an employer uses a particular test to identify a given set of abilities and aptitudes, these must be shown to be necessary to do the job. For example, it may need to be shown that high scorers do well in the job in question and that low scorers do not.

We mentioned the Sex Discrimination Act and the Race Relations Act. These two Acts, which have much in common, have identified two types of discrimination: direct and indirect. Direct discrimination is where an employer treats someone unfavourably or indeed favourably because of his or her sex, colour or ethnic background.

Such discrimination is unlawful. Indirect discrimination is where an employer sets a condition that a large proportion of a particular group fail to meet, eg, women or people from ethnic minority groups. This type of discrimination could be held to be unlawful if the condition set by the employer is not necessary or justified.

Why companies use tests

There are a number of advantages to companies and other organisations in using psychometric tests. These include:

1. Where an organisation receives a large number of applications, and because most selection tests are paper and pencil types, applicants can be tested in large groups. This, of course, is much more cost-effective.
2. The recruitment and selection process can be a costly affair, particularly if there is a high turnover of staff because of bad selection decisions, not to mention any other disruptions that may be caused. Thus it is in the interests of the company to choose the right people for the job. The use of tests can help in this process, provided that the tests are both valid and reliable.
3. Tests can also lessen subjectiveness in assessing the applicant's potential to develop his or her aptitude for a particular job. The lessening of subjectiveness in the selection process is also an advantage for applicants.
4. The use of tests with other selection procedures can lead to better and fairer decisions on the part of the employer.

Test conditions

Most tests are conducted under strict 'examination'-type conditions. The main reason for this is to ensure that all candidates, at all times, are tested in the same manner. This is so that no group being tested is either advantaged or disadvantaged in terms of receiving the test instructions.

The process followed will be laid down by the test publishers. However, the majority of tests are likely to be conducted in the following way:

1.   All candidates will be sitting facing the test administrator.
2.   Candidates will be provided with all the materials necessary, such as pencils, eraser, answer sheets, rough paper (if allowed by test publisher).
3.   The tester will explain the purpose of the test(s) and also inform candidates how the test will be conducted.
4.   The tester will read the instructions to be followed for the test. These instructions may also be written on the test booklet, in which case they should be read at the same time. In some tests the candidates are left to read the instructions by themselves. The reading time may be included in the test time or extra time may be given.
5.   For the majority of tests, if not all, there is a strict time limit that the tester will adhere to. The tester may use a stopwatch; don't be put off by this. Interest inventories and personality question-naires do not usually have a strict time limit, though candidates are asked to complete them as quickly as possible.
6.   Many tests have example questions. In some tests the candidates are asked to attempt these, while others have them already completed. In any case, their purpose is to ensure that the candi-dates understand what is required of them.
7.   In most tests, candidates are given the opportunity to ask ques-tions. If you do not understand what is required of you, you should seek clarification. You should not feel intimidated about asking questions, no matter how trivial the question may seem to you. The chances are that there are other people who have similar questions but who haven't plucked up enough courage to ask them. So the motto is – ask; you have nothing to lose!

How the results are interpreted

So far we have talked about different types of test. Now we need to address the issue of what happens once you have taken the test.

Naturally, they are scored; that is, they are marked. Once scored, the correct answers are added together. The result is called a raw score. If there is more than one test all the raw scores are noted. A set of tests is called a battery of tests.

The raw score does not really mean anything on its own. This is because it does not tell us whether it is a good or a bad score. Let us assume that candidate A gets 30 questions right out of a possible 50. So candidate A has a raw score of 30. If the test is easy and most people who are similar to him or her would have scored around 40, A's score is bad. On the other hand, if the test is a difficult one and most of the other people would only have scored around 20, candidate A's score is a good one.

Thus, in order for the scores to be meaningful, we have to compare the individual's score with that of a similar group of people. We would then be able to say that, compared to those people, this individual is either average, above average or below average. We make this comparison by using what are called norm tables. Norm tables tell us how other people have scored on a test. The group with whom we would compare an individual's score is called a norm group and test norms are the norm group's scores. In a norm referenced test the raw scores are compared with a norm group.

What to do if invited to sit a test

Why practice helps

If you and some friends were invited to enter a competition to change the wheel of a car in the shortest possible time and your team had practised, you would expect to be faster as a result. Your team would be less prone to mistakes and you would set about the task in a far more effective way.

Practice can lead to improvements in performance in most sorts of test, including those used by companies during selection. By how much your score might improve depends on a number of things. One is the amount of practice that you undertake; another is the quality of the material on which you practise (it must be similar to the real test). An important variable is whether you have had much previous experience of selection tests. The candidate who is new to tests stands to show the most improvement, while someone who has had lots of test experience may show little or no improvement.

The most important single factor that will decide by how much you improve your score through practice is you! To improve, you have to be motivated. From our experience, doing well in a selection test is not simply a matter of intelligence or aptitude: you also have to try hard and you must have a certain amount of self-confidence.

As we have said, not everyone will show an improvement; if you have taken lots of selection tests you may show little or none. Equally, anyone who is a poor reader or weak at maths may need to attend literacy or numeracy classes before any noticeable improvement. But for many, practice will make a significant contribution and in some cases will allow you to pass what you would otherwise have failed.

Whether practice will make the difference in a particular instance depends on where you are starting from. If you would have passed anyway, practice may only help you to obtain a slightly higher score. If you would have failed with a very low score, you may not be able to improve enough to pass, no matter how much you practise. However, you may be among the large number of candidates who fail a selection test by only a few marks and 12 to 16 hours' practice may mean that, instead of failing, you pass.

The way to look at it is this. What have you got to lose? Spending, say, two hours a night for six nights practising for a test can only help and it might make all the difference.

There is evidence to suggest that practice does help. For example, a woman who had twice failed the Civil Service test for Administrative Assistants, and had been trying to get an administrative job in the Civil Service for over a year, enrolled on a course that provided a total of five days' test practice. At the end of the course she sat the test and passed.

Make a decision

You have to decide how much you want the job. If you decide that it is something you really want you should make up your mind to attend the test! It is not unusual for as many as 40 per cent of the candidates to fail to show up on the day. You are also going to have to set aside some time to prepare for the test.

If, in your search for work, you have experienced a lot of rejection it is going to take courage to make the level of commitment that we ask.

Establish a clear idea of the test demands

The company or organisation that invites you to take a test will most likely include with the invitation a test description. This is an important source of information. If you do not receive such a description, telephone the company and ask if you can be sent details.

It is essential that you establish from the test description a clear idea of what the test involves and select exercises with similar demands. To help ensure that you do indeed have a clear idea, try the following exercise.

Familiarise yourself with the test description to the point at which you are able to describe in your own words each section of the test. For example, you ought to be able to state how many sections the test consists of, how long you are allowed for each section and what you have to do in each. If you are unable to do this you are not sufficiently familiar with the test description, so continue to read it to yourself until you can describe each section in your own words.

Ask someone else to read the description sent by the organisation and explain to him or her your account of what you are going to have to do. If your friend accepts your account of the test, you've got it.

Seek out relevant material

If the test involves maths and English exercises the majority of the material in this book will be of use. However, if the test is designed to measure, for example, coordination, dexterity, perceptual skills or abstract mental reasoning, you will need to obtain additional material. Likely sources are books with exercises purporting to measure IQ (intelligence quotient) or offering an assessment of aptitude. Libraries and career services may be able to lend you copies. If the test measures specialist knowledge seek out textbooks on the subject, especially those that end sections with questions and answers. Libraries of colleges of further education may be a good place to begin your search. If you are not a student you will probably not be allowed to borrow books, but no one should mind you using the library for reference purposes. You will find a list of further relevant titles from Kogan Page on pages 243–44.

Prepare a programme of work

Once you have a clear idea of the test demands and sufficient practice material you need to plan when and where you are to practise.

You should practise for no more than two hours at a time and allow some time fairly close to the test. The benefits of practice are short-lived so practise right up to the day before the test. Although some is better than none, you should aim to undertake a minimum of 12 hours, and perhaps as much as 20 hours, of practice. The factor that will probably decide how much practice you do will be the amount of relevant material that you can obtain.

Always work somewhere quiet and don't listen to music or watch television at the same time. Your programme of work ought to look something like this:

- You are notified that you are going to have to sit a test.
- You undertake a study of the test description (two hours).
- You search for relevant practice material.
- You undertake a series of two-hour practice sessions (10 to 18 hours).
- You take the test.

Coach yourself

Work through the material that you have obtained at your own pace without consulting the answers. Then go over it with the answers, trying to work out why the answer is the one given, rather than simply seeing how many you have got right; that way you are learning. Put the material aside and move on to other material; after a few days go through the original material again, this time against the clock (you might give yourself a minute an exercise). By following this method you will go over the material three times under a combination of conditions.

The night before the test

Lack of sleep or illness will affect your score detrimentally. You need to get a good night's sleep before the test. If you are unwell telephone the organisation to see if you can sit the test at a later date. Do not drink alcohol before a test.

Test anxiety

Do you get worried before taking a test? Do you tend to think you are not doing well while taking a test?

Test anxiety is quite a common problem for most people. The only difference is the degree to which people worry. Generally, it has been found that a slight amount of anxiety is a good thing; however a large amount can be detrimental.

Too much worry and too many negative thoughts can draw attention away from the task in hand – that of taking the test – and thereby disrupt performance. On the other hand, a little anxiety is beneficial: it will help you to be more alert and help your performance.

If you are one of those people who worry too much and have negative thoughts about your performance during a test, you will need to learn how to relax. You will also need to be more positive. After all, failing a test is not the end of the world – though it may seem like it at the time!

Test strategies

How you conduct yourself during the test is of utmost importance. There are a few golden rules.

Probably every test paper in the country advises the candidate against spending too long on a particular question. It is good advice. If you do not think you are going to be able to answer a question, move on to the next and if there is time come back to the questions that you have missed.

It is important that you place your answer in the correct place on the answer sheet or test booklet. If the test has an answer sheet separate from the questions, take particular care to check regularly that the question number corresponds to the number against your answer.

It is equally important that you indicate your chosen answer in the way requested. If the instructions ask you to, for example, tick the correct answer, make sure you do tick your choice rather than perhaps circle it or underline it.

Guessing sometimes pays. If the test is a multiple-choice paper and you do not know the answer, it may pay to guess. If, for example, you have to choose from four possible answers guessing would allow you to get, on average, one question in four right. Often you can improve on this average because you are sometimes able to recognise one or more of the suggested answers as incorrect.

Estimating sometimes helps in multiple-choice maths tests. Rather than working out inconvenient sums it is quicker if you round the amount up or down to a convenient number.

What to do if you fail

We have coached a lot of people through a range of selection tests and know for certain that failure does not necessarily mean that you are unable or do not have the ability to do the job. All it definitely means is that you failed the test! You may be perfectly able to do the job and pass the test if you took it a second or third time. The thing to do is not to give up.

Most companies will not tell you your score or allow you to retake the test straight away. In some cases you are not allowed to retake the test for six months and you will have to re-apply, which involves filling out the application form, and so on, all over again. This means that you have time to improve your English or maths so that you pass the test the next time.

It will help if, straight after the test, you sit down and try to remember as many of the questions as you can. Then go and find some exercises that remind you of the test. We suggested earlier the kinds of place you might find them.

Now test yourself on the examples that you managed to find; try to be honest and, if you do really badly, it may be that the only way you are going to improve is to attend classes at a college of further education. If you attended for a year you might obtain sufficient qualifications to exempt you from having to do the test again!

Some of the most common types of test

In this chapter, descriptions are given of some of the most common kinds of test and their demands are illustrated with examples. Further practice material is provided in Chapter 5.

You are most likely to encounter the following types of test:

- *Verbal reasoning.* These are about how well you understand ideas expressed in words and how you think and reason with words.
- *Numerical reasoning.* Like the verbal tests these aim to identify strengths in understanding, only in this case it is your strength in understanding and reasoning with numbers.
- *Diagrammatic reasoning.* These deal with diagrams.
- *Mechanical reasoning.* These deal with mechanical concepts.
- *Abstract reasoning.* These seek to identify how good you are at thinking in abstract terms, ie, dealing with problems that are not presented in a verbal or numerical format.
- *Clerical skills.* These deal with checking and classifying data, speedily and accurately.

All the practice material provided in this book relates to the verbal, numerical and clerical types of test. If you are interested in diagrammatic tests of reasoning, you will find practice material in the following two books useful: *How to Pass Computer Selection Tests* and *How to Pass Technical Selection Tests* (both published by Kogan Page).

Nearly all these tests will have a time limit. But we have not imposed time constraints in this chapter because it is more important that you become familiar with the tests, and this is best done under relaxed conditions where you work at your own pace. Later you will find exercises that allow you to practise against time.

Verbal tests

Tests that measure comprehension

These tests set out to establish if the candidate can demonstrate a level of understanding of written language. They can involve, for example, swapping or finding missing words, choosing between sentences, or identifying words that have the same or opposite meaning.

Tests that assess spelling

Most spelling tests require you to indicate which words in a list are incorrectly spelt. In some cases you are provided with a list of correctly spelt words from which you are able to check the spelling. You may have either to write or underline the correct spelling or look the word up on a correctly spelt list and write down the corresponding number.

Tests of grammar and punctuation

Grammar demonstrates the relations between words, while punctuation serves to divide and emphasise. It is quite common for tests of grammar and punctuation to examine also your command of spelling and comprehension.

Tests of logical thinking

These tests are intended to measure the candidate's ability to follow instructions or work out relationships between numbers, shapes, figures or statements and predict, for example, what comes next.

Numerical tests

The purpose of these tests is to examine your grasp of the four funda-
mental operations of arithmetic: addition, subtraction, multiplication
and division. We later refer to these as the four rules. Sometimes the
test also investigates the candidate's handling of percentages and fractions. You are not usually allowed to use a calculator, slide rule or any
other sort of aid. These tests may also require the candidates to apply
their grasp of arithmetic to a series of practical situations or demonstrate their understanding by estimating the answers.

Tests of clerical and computing skills

There are many tests that try to predict whether a candidate is suited
to work with computers or as a clerk. For example, the tests inves-
tigate the candidate's ability to check information, follow coded
instructions or rules, sequence events into a logical order and interpret
flow diagrams.

Practice examples

The following pages provide practice examples of some of the most
common types of test. Do not worry if you cannot do some of the
examples. If you get stuck ask someone to help. Answers are given on
pages 196–99.

1.   Verbal tests that measure comprehension

A.   Swapping words

Comprehension tests sometimes consist of single sentences or pairs of
sentences that either do not read sensibly or have a word or words
missing. You have to make the sentences sensible by swapping words
or you have to complete a sentence by choosing words from a list.

Examples of swapping words:

Tick the two words that if swapped would make the following sensible.

> you have to try test to do well in a hard.

Note that in this type of test you must only switch two words and from wherever you move the first word the other must go. Sometimes the question consists of two sentences, one of which requires no revision.

Now try this example:

Tick the two words that if swapped would make the following sensible.

> limit all tests impose a time virtually

B.   Finding missing words

If the sentence has a word or words missing you are expected to indicate which word or words are needed to complete the sentence, usually from a number of suggestions.

Examples of missing words:

> The. . . sat on the. . .

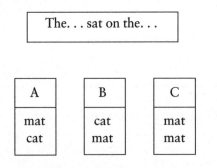

A	B	C
mat cat	cat mat	mat mat

Answer

C.   Locating words that mean the same or the opposite

Comprehension-type selection tests sometimes test a candidate's grasp of synonyms (words in the same language that mean the same) or antonyms (words that mean the opposite of each other or are contradictory). For example:

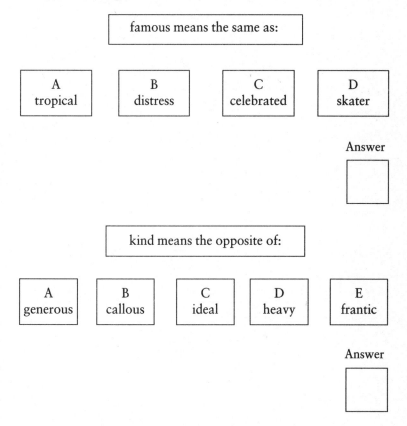

famous means the same as:

| A tropical | B distress | C celebrated | D skater |

Answer

kind means the opposite of:

| A generous | B callous | C ideal | D heavy | E frantic |

Answer

2.   Tests of grammar and punctuation

These tests often involve the candidate having to choose which of a number of sentences are correct or, alternatively, choose from a number of words, or pairs of words, which will correctly complete a sentence.

A.   Choosing from a number of sentences

In each of the following two examples, choose which sentence is correct and place its letter label in the answer box.

> (a) Where would you go to buy shoes.
>
> (b) Where would you go to buy shoe?
>
> (c) Where would you go to buy shoes?
>
> (d) Where would you go to buy shoe's?

Answer

> (a) A yacht is a type of boat that has sails.
>
> (b) A yacht is a type of boat which that sails.
>
> (c) A yacht is a type of boat who has sails.
>
> (d) A yacht is a type of boat who that sails.

Answer

B. Choosing from pairs of words

Choose which pair of words correctly fits the spaces in the incomplete sentence.

Thomas and . . . visit you yesterday.

A	B	C	D
me will	I will	me did	I did

Answer

Try this example:

. . . were . . . policemen to every protester.

A	B	C	D
Their too	There to	Their two	There two

Answer

3. Spelling tests

These tests require you to identify which words are either correctly or incorrectly spelt. Sometimes you have to write out the correct spelling or underline either those correctly or incorrectly spelt. It is important that you pay attention to the instructions otherwise you may make the error of, for example, underlining the correct spellings when you were asked to underline the incorrect ones. Try the following examples:

Example 1.   Underline the *correct* spellings.

Wedesday	Febuary	indecate	butiful
sincerely	foreign	sataday	archetec
immediate	equiped	merchandise	juvenille
deliverys	mashinery	shampoo	responcibility

Example 2.   Where the spelling is wrong write the correct spelling in the space alongside.

author	....	balence	....
beeutify	....	corelate	....
desease	....	foremost	....
holiday	....	occasion	....

Example 3.   Below is a list of 25 words, spelt correctly and in alphabetical order. There then follow two groups of seven words. In each of these groups there may be up to three spelling errors. Your task is to find the word or words that are incorrectly spelt. Once you have found these words, locate them in the first list in which spellings are correct and write their numbers in the answer box. Your answers do not have to be in numerical order. One of the answers has been given.

List

1. among	11. hasten	21. warranty
2. balance	12. hypocrisy	22. writing
3. calendar	13. imprecise	23. yield
4. creative	14. knuckle	24. yourself
5. delayed	15. league	25. zeal
6. disturb	16. numerous	
7. emphasis	17. plasticity	
8. equality	18. receive	
9. forgery	19. secretary	
10. generous	20. vacuum	

1.

calendar	hypocrisy
recieve	balance
amoung	vacum
yourself	

Answer

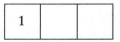

1		

2.

zeal	warrantie
delaiyded	generous
plasticity	hasten
secretery	

Answer

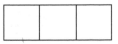

4.   Tests of logical thinking

Sometimes you have to follow instructions in this type of test or you may be expected to work out relationships and then make a prediction.

A.   Following instructions

There are a wide number of variations on this type of test. The instructions you have to follow often include the alphabet and numbers. These types of question may or may not be multiple-choice. Here is a useful tip: with this sort of question it helps if you take one clause at a time. Try these examples:

Example 1

If Wednesday comes before Friday and May comes before December, place the second letter of the alphabet in the answer box. Otherwise place the first letter of the word Wednesday in the answer box.

Answer

Example 2

Divide the largest figure by the smallest and then add the result to the second figure from the left. Enter the letter that matches your result in the answer box.

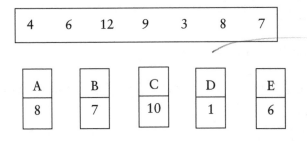

| 4 | 6 | 12 | 9 | 3 | 8 | 7 |

A	B	C	D	E
8	7	10	1	6

Answer

B.   Relationships between numbers and statements

In this sort of question you have to say what you think logically fits the gap or will come next. Sometimes you are expected to identify which is the odd one out from a collection of numbers, words or shapes. Try these examples:

Example 1.   What number fits the gap?

> 7   11 ... 19   23

Answer

Example 2.   Which is the odd one out?

> (a)   The Isle of Wight
>
> (b)   Anglesey
>
> (c)   Skye
>
> (d)   Stoke on Trent

Answer

Example 3.   Which is the odd one out?

| 5 | 25 | 16 | 40 |

Answer

Example 4.   Which is the odd one out?

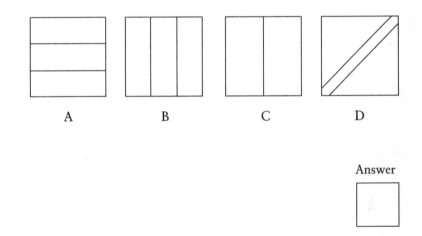

A   B   C   D

Answer

5.   Numerical tests

Most numeracy tests require you to complete a variety of sums that will test your command of the four rules: addition, subtraction, multiplication and division. Try the following examples without using a calculator. Do not worry if you get stuck; there are lots more practice examples given later in the book.

A.   The four rules

1. Add
    980054
    60273
    _____ Answer

2. Subtract
    607389
    236571
    _____ Answer

3. Add each line below and
    then subtract the smaller answer
    from the greater.

    $5 + 17 + 5 =$
    $12 + 6 + 11 =$

    _____
    _____ Answer

4. Divide
                    _____ Answer
    $12 \overline{\smash{)}4920}$

5. Multiply

    50746
    26

    _____ Answer

6. Multiply each line
    below and then divide
    the lesser answer
    into the greater.

    $6 \times 40 =$
    $4 \times 3 =$

                    Answer

Make sure that your answers are in the correct place.

B.   Practical numerical problems
Some companies are concerned that you can not only carry out basic
mathematical calculations but also apply them in practical situations.
To test this ability they use the following kinds of question.

Example 1

If a first class stamp costs 30 pence, how much would 50 first class stamps cost?

Answer

Example 2

If the balance of petty cash is £93.70 before you were instructed to purchase stationery to the value of £20.18 what would be the new balance?

Answer

Example 3

Fourteen people attended the annual office party and the cost was £350. How much is that per head?

Answer

Example 4

The office photocopier service contract is charged at 1.4 pence each copy. How much would be charged for 1500 copies?

Answer

C.   Estimating/approximating

This type of test sets out to measure your ability to approximate the answer to calculations. Usually, this type of test is multiple-choice and the amount of time allowed does not allow you to work out answers exactly. Try these examples:

Example 1

48 + 55 =

1113		33		203		103		93
A		B		C		D		E

Answer

Example 2

12 × 9 =

108		78		128		1108
A		B		C		D

Answer

D.   Percentages and fractions

In addition to the four rules discussed and illustrated above, some tests also examine your command of fractions and percentages. The questions may take any of the forms so far covered. For example:

Example 1

$$\frac{1}{2} + \frac{2}{3} + \frac{1}{4} =$$

Example 2

$$\frac{1}{4} + 2\frac{1}{3} + \frac{1}{2} =$$

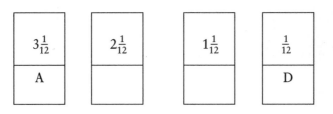

$3\frac{1}{12}$	$2\frac{1}{12}$	$1\frac{1}{12}$	$\frac{1}{12}$
A			D

Answer

Example 3

> Your employer asked if you would work overtime at time and a half. Your normal rate of pay was £4.50 an hour. How much an hour would you earn while working overtime?

Answer

Example 4

The cost of a new fax machine was £640 without value added tax. If the tax was 17.5%, how much would the total cost of the fax machine be?

Answer

Example 5

What is 24% of £380?

Answer

Example 6

Estimate 65% of 350. Enter the letter corresponding to your answer in the box.

508	227.5	58	1208
A	B	C	D

Answer

6.   Tests of clerical and computing skills

These tests attempt to measure a candidate's aptitude for computing and clerical work. You may have to sit them as part of a battery of tests that could include verbal and numerical tests as described above. They include following coded instructions, interpreting flow diagrams, suggesting the appropriate sequence of events, and checking that data has been accurately inputted. Try the following examples:

A.   Flow diagrams

Flow diagrams are used to represent a sequence of events, their interconnections and outcomes. Study the flow diagram below; it represents the opening of a computer file. Use it to answer the question.

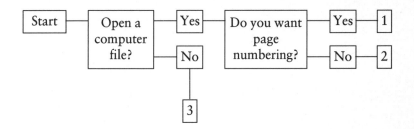

Question
A user wishes to open a file without page numbering. Which outcome does the user require: 1, 2 or 3?

Answer

B.   Sequencing

These are tests in which you have to put a set of items or instructions into a defined order. Sometimes the items are everyday things like going to work or they may be particular to computing. Try the following:

Write what you believe is the correct order for these events in the answer box.

Word processing

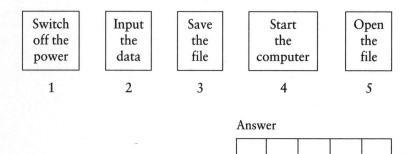

Switch off the power	Input the data	Save the file	Start the computer	Open the file
1	2	3	4	5

Answer

C.   Coded instructions

This type of question involves sets of rules that you have to interpret and then apply. Try the following example:

Below are a set of codes and their meanings. You have to use this information to answer the series of questions.

Code

To open a file	OF	To check the spelling in a file	SP
To copy a file	CF		
To leave the program	ESC	To save a file	SF
To delete a file	DF		

Questions

What is the code:

1.   To open a file?   Answer

2.   To delete a file and leave the program?   Answer

3.   To open a file, check the spelling and save the file?   Answer

D. Checking computer data

In these tests you are provided with both the original information and a computer printout. You have to check to see whether the data has been accurately inputted on to the computer files.

Example:

In this example you have to check line by line the computer data against the original. If you find any discrepancies mark the answer box with the letter N; if the line has been accurately copied mark the box with the letter Y.

The answer to the first example has been given below.

Original information

1	Land Sales Ltd	9 Lancia Place	Lancaster Gate	ES2 5HJ
2	Fox Associates	143 West Side	Ealing	5HJ 6TT
3	Colliers Building	68 Cambridge Street	Queens Way	3DD 5TG
4	Top Creation	11 George Road	Plaistow	9NN 4RF
5	Victoria Packing Systems	34a Major Street	Great Hardwood	2DE 6VC
6	Municipal Supplies	22 Warehouse Road	Small Heath	8MN 6AS
7	Berton Hotel	78 Baker Street	Uxbridge	12FD 5TT
8	Save Finance	53 Church Yard Close	Sherman	7FC 4DX
9	Longsdale Ltd	2 Burton Street	Hackney	E5 2CD
10	Western Electronics	10 Resister Road	East Ham	E6 4RF
11	New Technologies	13 Fourth Avenue	Manor Park	E12 5NT
12	Net Surfing Cafe	20 Cyber Street	Compton	CB13 7FG
13	Super Robotics Plc	145 Wells Street	High Grove	HG8 2WL
14	Info Tech Ltd	1 New Lane	Hertfordshire	NW3 2SA
15	Printer Printers	2 Print Street	Printington	PT5 2PR

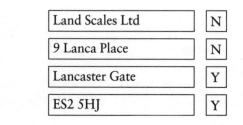

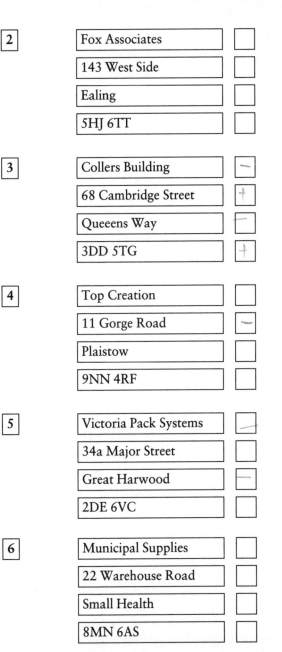

2	Fox Associates	
	143 West Side	
	Ealing	
	5HJ 6TT	

3	Collers Building	—
	68 Cambridge Street	＋
	Queeens Way	—
	3DD 5TG	＋

4	Top Creation	
	11 Gorge Road	—
	Plaistow	
	9NN 4RF	

5	Victoria Pack Systems	—
	34a Major Street	
	Great Harwood	—
	2DE 6VC	

6	Municipal Supplies	
	22 Warehouse Road	
	Small Health	
	8MN 6AS	

7

Barton Hotel	
78 Baker Street	
Uxbrige	
12DD 5TT	

8

Save Finances	
53 Church Yard Close	
Sherman	
7FC 4DX	

9

Longsdale LTD	
2 Burton Street	
Hackney	
E5 2CD	

10

Western Electronic	
10 Resister Rood	
EastHam	
E9 4RF	

11

New Technology	
13 Forth Avenue	
Manor Park	
E12 5NT	

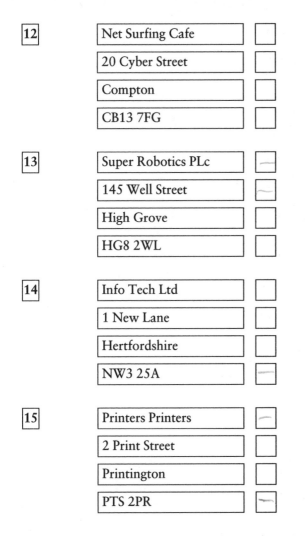

12	Net Surfing Cafe	☐
	20 Cyber Street	☐
	Compton	☐
	CB13 7FG	☐

13	Super Robotics PLc	☐
	145 Well Street	☐
	High Grove	☐
	HG8 2WL	☐

14	Info Tech Ltd	☐
	1 New Lane	☐
	Hertfordshire	☐
	NW3 25A	☐

15	Printers Printers	☐
	2 Print Street	☐
	Printington	☐
	PTS 2PR	☐

When you check your answers, go over the exercises that you got wrong again and see if you can work out your mistake.

Practice material

This chapter consists of practice exercises relevant to some of the most common types of test currently used for selection purposes. The exercises are divided into three categories: verbal, numerical and clerical.

Time limits have been suggested for some of the exercises and answers can be found on pages 200–16. When you check your answers try not to see simply how many questions you got right; instead, go back over the questions and try to work out why you went wrong. That way you are learning.

Verbal tests

1.   The same meaning or the opposite

Underline the word that has the same meaning and circle the word that has the opposite meaning as the first word on the *left*. For example:

elastic	brittle	hidden	<u>stretchy</u>	action

Try these:

store	stockpile	sieve	tent	waste
wrong	nail	catch	mistaken	right
question	answer	misery	describe	enquire
measure	artery	volume	guess-work	gauge

problem	absent	concave	solution	obstacle
obscure	objective	transparent	conceal	
synthetic	man-made	music	thought	natural
vertical	horizontal	upright	topmost	
repair	impair	neglect	recondition	test
strengthen	lengthen	purify	augment	weaken

If you do not know the answers to any of these examples look them up in a dictionary. You could also try a Thesaurus, which lists synonyms (words that mean the same). Once you have finished the exercise, why not make up some examples of your own?

Your grasp of synonyms and opposites may be tested in a variety of ways. Here are some examples of the way these types of question are worded. Try them and make up examples of your own.

You have to underline the correct answer.

1.   Car is to motor boat as bike is to:

> pedalo   rowing boat   sailing boat   submarine

Now make up an example of this type of question yourself:

_____ is to _____ as _____ is to:

2.   Skill means the same as:

> weak ability inept cunning

Make up an example of this type of question:
_____ means the same as:
_____ _____ _____ _____

3.   Which of the following means fight?

brute   burn   brawn   brawl

Make an example:

Which of the following means _____?

_____ _____ _____ _____

4.   Hard is to soft as stone is to:

rock   water   mud   marble

Make up an example of this kind of question:

_____ is to _____ as _____ is to:

5.   Long means the opposite of:

high   low   short   wide

Make up an example yourself:

_____ means the opposite of:

_____ _____ _____ _____

2.   Sound alike/look alike words

Some words have different meanings but sound identical or very similar, for example:

site (place) and sight (view)

Other words again have different meanings but look similar, for example:

dairy (milking shed) and diary (memoir)

Words that sound or look like other words are often used in verbal selection tests and it is surprising how often the same examples come up. It may help if you are clear over the difference between the meaning of some common examples.

Use a dictionary if necessary to be clear about the difference in meaning between the pairs of words below. Then make up sentences that demonstrate the difference. For example, in the case of site and sight:

Sentence 1.   The site is over on the left.

Sentence 2.   It rained all the way and by the time they arrived they were quite a sight.

Now write a sentence for the word 'cite', which also sounds like site and sight.

Sentence 3. _____

_____

Be sure you understand the difference in meaning of these sound alike/look alike words.

Exercise 1

morning mourning	ascent assent	principal principle
be bee	here hear	edition addition
whether weather	right write	piece peace
course cause	except accept	brake break
specific Pacific	meet meat	advise advice
boar bore	allowed aloud	excess access
effect affect	council counsel	though through threw
practice practise	waist waste	for fore four
stationary stationery	there their	

You have **two** minutes in which to place the correct pairs of words from the above lists into the gaps in the sentences below.

1. We. . . . . . . down on him.
   The. . . . . . . was in the cage next to the elephant.

2. You need to be more. . . . . . . in the use of your words.
   We looked out across the. . . . . . . Ocean.

3. He went this. . . . . . .
   She is in. . . . . . .

4. It was the. . . . . . . of the matter.
   We had to do it, after all she was the. . . . . . .

5. I was up to my. . . . . . . in it.
   It seemed so wrong that there was so much. . . . . . .

6. . . . . . . I waited for over half an hour.
   The sound of some words gives an indication of. . . . . . . meaning.

Exercise 2

You are presented with a number of sentences. In each sentence you will find two or more words placed in brackets. Your task is to choose one word that best completes the sentence and write it in the space provided.

1. All the guests (knew, new) each other at the party.

   . . . .

2. There was (to, too, two) much traffic on the motorway.

   . . . .

3. In a South American country the (guerrillas, gorillas) were on the verge of gaining control of the capital city.

   . . . .

4. The (rap, wrap) on the door caused John to awaken from his dream.

   . . . .

5. There were only a (few, phew) television sets left in the shop.

   . . . .

6. Louise was asked to collect the (draft, draught) from the bank on her way to work.

   . . . .

7. It was all (quiet, quite) on the Western Front.

   . . . .

8. All the (writes, rights, rites) were performed by the local priest.

   . . . .

9. That building was built in the 17th century and was originally an (arms, alms) house.

   . . . .

10. In the old days, water pipes were made from (led, lead).

    . . . .

11. The gale force wind was (effecting, affecting) the television reception.

    . . . .

12. They found it difficult to decide (whether, weather) to go to Spain or to France for the holiday.

. . . .

13. The lorry driver (accepted, excepted) that it was his fault.

. . . .

14. It was a great (feet, feat) that the climbers achieved.

. . . .

15. She placed the bottles over (there, their, they're) on the table.

. . . .

16. To quote is to (cite, site, sight).

. . . .

17. The computer should not be switched (of, off) until the disk has been removed.

. . . .

18. The surgery was full of (patients, patience) waiting to see the doctor.

. . . .

19. The postman put the letters (through, threw) the letterbox.

. . . .

20. At the interview Jane was asked to take a (sit, seat).

. . . .

21. Children should be seen and not (heard, herd).

. . . .

22. Kathy said her voice felt very (horse, hoarse).

. . . .

23. The postman always brings the (male, mail) at 8.30.

. . . .

24. The (scene, seen) from the hill top was magnificent.

   . . . .

25. Everyone went to the party (accept, except) James.

   . . . .

26. When the phone rang, Jane and Chris were on (there, their, they're) way out to the shops.

   . . . .

3.   Choosing the right word

In many verbal tests you have to choose a word from a number of options that you believe completes the sentence correctly. Try the following examples:

Instructions
You have to choose a word from the box that in your opinion correctly completes the sentence, then write that word in the space.

1.   I left the car over _____.

> there, their

2.   I could not have _____ another thing.

> eaten, ate

3.   _____ the post arrived yet?

> has, have

4.   It looks _____ it is going to rain.

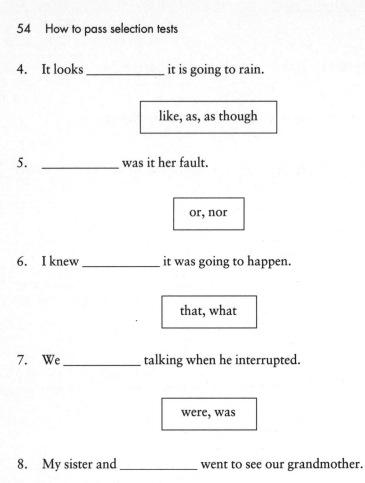

| like, as, as though |

5.   _____ was it her fault.

| or, nor |

6.   I knew _____ it was going to happen.

| that, what |

7.   We _____ talking when he interrupted.

| were, was |

8.   My sister and _____ went to see our grandmother.

| me, I |

4.   Timed exercise – choosing the right word

Over the page you will find 10 questions. Before you turn over, set a clock or watch to allow yourself **five** minutes to complete them.

Instructions
Choose from the suggested answers the words that you believe correctly complete the sentence and write them in the space provided. It could be a question of either spelling, grammar or meaning.

Do not turn the page to begin the timed exercise until you are ready.

1.   They all _____ that she was _____.

> knew, leave, new, gnu, leaving, leafing

2.   _____ should _____ seen them.

> ewe, you, had, have

3.   She is a very _____ young _____.

> abel, able, women, woman

4.   I do hope the _____ will be _____.

> weather, whether, fine, fined

5.   We _____ _____ this morning.

> flew, flu, flue, accross, across

6.   We must _____ to _____.

> agreement, agree, agreed, differ, difer

7. My eyes are _____ from looking at the _____ screen.

> tied, tyred, tired, colour, colore

8. The results are given in the _____ and _____ below.

> colum, column, rows, roes, rouse

9. Can this _____ be _____ on our computer?

> program, programme, uses, used

10. The _____ _____ called and asked if you would phone back.

> centre, centaur, manger, manager

END OF EXERCISE

5. Choosing the right sentence

Sometimes verbal tests require you to choose a sentence rather than a particular word. This type of test can examine your command of punctuation as well as grammar, spelling and syntax (meaning). Try the following examples:

1.

A. I thought that their was a problem with the laser printer?
B. I thought that there was a problem with the laser printer.
C. I through that their was a problem with the laser printer.
D. I through that they're was a problem with the laser printer.

Answer

2.

A. The matter will be given immediate attention.
B. The matter will be given mediate attention.
C. The matter will be given mediate attension.

Answer

3.

A. In response to the interest you have expressed in our product I enclose the relevant information, order form and price list.
B. In responce to the interest you have expressed in our product I enclose, the relevant information, order form and price list.
C. In responce to the interest you have expressed in our product I enclose the relevant information order form and pice list.

Answer

4.

A.   The most common form of dismissal involves the termination of a worker's contract with notice.
B.   The most common form of dismissal involves the termination of a workers' contract with notice.
C.   The most common form of dismissal involves the termination of a workers contract with notice.

Answer

5.

A   Childcare facilties have being made available.
B.   Childcare facility have been made available.
C.   Childcare facilities have been made available.
D.   Childcare facilities has been made available.

Answer

Here is a useful tip: it helps if you not only look for the correct answer but also try to rule out some of the sentences by recognising them as incorrect.

Over the page are 10 further examples of this type of question. Check your watch and allow yourself **five** minutes to complete them.

Do not turn the page to begin the timed exercise until you are ready.

6.   Timed exercise – choosing the right sentence

1.

A.   There is the man whom represents the company.
B.   There is the man which represents the company.
C.   There is the man who represents the company.
D.   There is the man what represents the company.

Answer

2.

A.   Luckily the error was discovered before the end of the physical year.
B.   Luckily the error was discovered before the end of the fiscal year.
C.   Luckily the era was discovered before the end of the fiscal year.
D.   Luckily the era was discovered before the end of the physical.

Answer

3.

A.   In the enclosed envelop you will find the reciept.
B.   In the enclosed envelope you will find the receipt.
C.   In the enclosed envelope you will find the reciept.
D.   In the enclosed envelop you will find the receipt.

Answer

4.

A. David said John is late.
B. 'David said' John is late.
C. David said, 'John is late.'
D. David, 'said John', is late.

Answer

5.

A. The committee sat much later than expected.
B. The comittee sat much latter than expected.
C. The committee sat much later than accept.
D. The committe sat much later than expected.

Answer

6.

A. I like Fridays and I hate Mondays.
B. I like Fridays both I hate Mondays.
C. I like Fridays nor I hate Mondays.
D. I like Fridays but I like Mondays.

Answer

7.

A.   There really is an access of filing to be done.
B.   There really is an excess of fileing to be done.
C.   There really is an access of fileing to be done.
D.   There really is an excess of filing to be done.

Answer

8.

A.   Try not to allow your expenditure to exceed what you urn.
B.   Try not to allow your expenditure to accede what you earn.
C.   Try not to allow your expenditure to exceed what you earn.
D.   Try not to allow your expenditure to excess what you earn.

Answer

9.

A.   Colin was born on the 19th August, at King Street Hospital Manchester, his father was at work.
B.   Colin was born on the 19th August, at king street hospital Manchester his father was at work.
C.   Colin was Born on the 19th August at King Street Hospital manchester his Father was at Work.
D.   Colin was born on the 19th August at King Street hospital Manchester his father was at work.
E.   Colin was born on the 19th August, at King Street Hospital, Manchester; his father was at work.

Answer

10.

A. The delivery of stationary is two days late.
B. The delivery of stationery is too days late.
C. The delivery of stationary is to days late.
D. The delivery of stationery is two days late.

Answer

END OF EXERCISE

You might find it useful to go back over these exercises at your own pace.

7.   Plural words

You are given a word for which you have to find the correct plural spelling from a list on the right-hand side. Now try this and see how you get on.

1. Interview   A. Interviewees
                       B. Interviewers
                       C. Interviews
                       D. Interviewes
                       E. None of these

2. Vacancy   A. Vacancys
                       B. Vacancyes
                       C. Vacancise
                       D. Vacancies
                       E. None of these

3. Shelf   A. Shelfs
                       B. Shelves
                       C. Shelfes
                       D. Shelvses
                       E. None of these

4. Match
A. Matchees
B. Matches
C. Matcheses
D. Matchses
E. None of these

5. Business
A. Business
B. Businesses
C. Businessis
D. Businessies
E. None of these

6. Monkey
A. Monkees
B. Monkeyes
C. Monkeies
D. Monkies
E. None of these

7. Family
A. Familys
B. Familyes
C. Familese
D. Families
E. None of these

8 Message
A. Messages
B. Messagess
C. Messagies
D. Messagees
E. None of these

9. Donkey
A. Donkeyes
B. Donkeyies
C. Donkeies
D. Donkies
E. None of these

10. Photocopy
A. Photocopis
B. Photocopyes
C. Photocopyis
D. Photocopies
E. None of these

11. Ability
   A. Abilitys
   B. Abilityes
   C. Abilites
   D. Abilities
   E. None of these

12. Capacity
   A. Capacites
   B. Capacitis
   C. Capaciteis
   D. Capacities
   E. None of these

13. Adjective
   A. Adjectives
   B. Adjectivies
   C. Adjectivees
   D. Adjectivyes
   E. None of these

14. Allegory
   A. Allegores
   B. Allegories
   C. Allegoryes
   D. Allegoryies
   E. None of these

15. Ambiguity
   A. Ambiguities
   B. Ambiguityes
   C. Ambiguitys
   D. Ambiguites
   E. None of these

16. Antique
   A. Antiquies
   B. Antiques
   C. Antiqueys
   D. Antiqueis
   E. None of these

17. Customer
   A. Customeres
   B. Customerse
   C. Customers
   D. Customeries
   E. None of these

18. Disguise
    A. Disguises
    B. Disguisees
    C. Disguisess
    D. Disguisies
    E. None of these

19. Euphemism
    A. Euphemismes
    B. Euphemisms
    C. Euphemismse
    D. Euphemismies
    E. None of these

20. Hoof
    A. Hoofs
    B. Hoovs
    C. Hoofes
    D. Hooves
    E. None of these

21. Guarantee
    A. Guaranteies
    B. Guaranteses
    C. Guarantees
    D. Guaranteis
    E. None of these

22. Machine
    A. Machinies
    B. Machines
    C. Machinees
    D. Machins
    E. None of these

23. Negative
    A. Negatives
    B. Negativeis
    C. Negativies
    D. Negativees
    E. None of these

24. Personality
    A. Personalities
    B. Personalites
    C. Personalitees
    D. Personalityes
    E. None of these

25. Platitude

A. Platituds
B. Platitudes
C. Platitudus
D. Platitudas
E. None of these

26. Psychologist

A. Psychologistes
B. Psychologists
C. Psychologisties
D. Psychologistees
E. None of these

27. Rhyme

A. Rhymies
B. Rhymes
C. Rhymses
D. Rhymeies
E. None of these

28. Sequence

A. Sequences
B. Sequencees
C. Sequenceies
D. Sequencies
E. None of these

29. Taxi

A. Taxies
B. Taxis
C. Taxise
D. Taxes
E. None of these

30. Roof

A. Roofs
B. Roovs
C. Roofes
D. Rooves
E. None of these

31. Sense

A. Senseces
B. Sencees
C. Sensies
D. Sensees
E. None of these

32. Thief
   A. Thiefes
   B. Thieves
   C. Thievse
   D. Thiefves
   E. None of these

33. Statesman
   A. Statesmans
   B. Statesmens
   C. Statesmen
   D. Statesman
   E. None of these

34. Technology
   A. Technologyes
   B. Technologies
   C. Technologys
   D. Technologees
   E. None of these

35. Language
   A. Languagies
   B. Languagees
   C. Languagese
   D. Language's
   E. None of these

8.   Spelling

Below is a list of 75 words, spelt correctly and in alphabetical order.

On the following pages you will find groups of nine words. In each group there may be up to four spelling errors. Your task is to find the word or words that are incorrectly spelt. Once you have found these words, locate them in the first list in which spellings are correct and write their numbers in the answer box. Your answers do not have to be in numerical order.

For your assistance an example has been given. Study the example and then complete the eight questions.

1. Abbreviate	26. Earring	51. Illustrate
2. Absolute	27. Economically	52. Impatient
3. Accountant	28. Egalitarian	52. Inadmissible
4. Alternative	29. Eligible	54. Incompatible
5. Autumn	30. Emperor	55. Inflammable
6. Beautiful	31. Equilibrium	56. Jostle
7. Beneficial	32. Exaggerate	57. Junction
8. Billiards	33. Failure	58. Ladder
9. Boutique	34. February	59. Language
10. Broadcast	35. Fiction	60. Laughter
11. Brutus	36. Flotation	61. Leadership
12. Bustle	37. Formula	62. Magistrate
13. Canada	38. Functionalism	63. Manage
14. Carburettor	39. Gallon	64. Marginal
15. Category	40. Geometric	65. Mercury
16. Caterpillar	41. Gesture	66. Middle
17. Centrifugal	42. Goggle	67. Minimum
18. Complementary	43. Gradual	68. Monetary
19. Definite	44. Graphology	69. Napkin
20. Defeatism	45. Handkerchief	70. Neighbour
21. Designer	46. Harbour	71. Nightingale
22. Develop	47. Hexagon	72. Northern
23. Devotee	48. Homogenous	73. Nucleus
24. Diffidence	49. Hospital	74. Numerous
25. Diplomatically	50. Humiliate	75. Nurture

For example:

Brodcast	Fiction	Leadership
Handkerchief	Formular	Earing
Hospital	Napkin	Hexagon

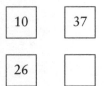

In this example there are only three errors, but as explained there can be up to four.

1.

Minnimum	Gradual	Centriugal
Deffinite	Northern	Jostle
Exaggerate	Defeatism	Homegenous

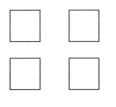

2.

Absolute	Ecconomically	Benefitial
Brutus	Napkin	Fiction
Ladder	Goggle	Mercury

3.

Language	Boutique	Failure
Gallon	Gestture	Devotee
Impatient	Febuary	Nurture

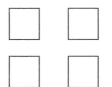

4.

Busle   Caterpillar   Complementary
Desiner   Humiliate   Marginal
Harbor   Manage   Canada

5.

Laughter   Graphology   Flotation
Geometric   Catagory   Deffinite
Hospital   Nightingale   Middle

6.

Egaletarian   Josle   Develop
Homogenous   Nucleaus   Accountant
Canada   Illustrate   Inflamable

7.

Autum	Harbour	Neighbour
Defaetism	Emparor	Ladder
Billiards	Gallon	Numerious

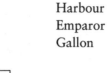

8.

Failure	Minnimum	Nightingale
Devalop	Humiliate	Northern
Mercurey	Carburettor	Difidence

9.   Timed spelling

Over the page are 10 further examples of this type of question. Check your watch and allow yourself **10** minutes to complete them.

Do not turn the page to begin the timed exercise until you are ready.

1. Alternate	26. Knife	51. Quintillion
2. Amalgamation	27. Kitchen	52. Radiate
3. Anaesthesia	28. Lagging	53. Rampage
4. Analogous	29. Latitude	54. Rapture
5. Appeasement	30. League	55. Recital
6. Arbitrary	31. Magazine	56. Rendezvous
7. Assessor	32. Mansion	57. Ridiculous
8. Broach	33. Minister	58. Safeguard
9. Bullion	34. Nitrate	59. Satellite
10. Ceremonious	35. Nominate	60. Scaffolding
11. Chancellor	36. Numeration	61. Scientist
12. Dismantle	37. Nutritious	62. Scratch
13. Diversity	38. Oath	63. Segregate
14. Exhaustion	39. Obsession	64. Solemnize
15. Expedient	40. Omission	65. Tangible
16. Flippant	41. Orchestra	66. Technician
17. Frustrate	42. Pantomime	67. Temporarily
18. Genealogy	43. Parochial	68. Tongue
19. Guillotine	44. Penicillin	69. Undulate
20. Hereditable	45. Petition	70. Utility
21. Humility	46. Pneumonia	71. Variety
22. Indentation	47. Pygmy	72. Velvet
23. Invention	48. Quadrangle	73. Warranty
24. Journal	49. Quicken	74. Wealthiness
25. Justify	50. Quinine	75. Xylophone

1.

Alternate	Broch	Petition
Neumonia	Pigme	Tongue
Rampage	League	Minister

2.

Flippant	Justify	Outh
Valwet	Asessor	Quicken
Safegard	Rapture	Invention

3.

Exhustion	Kitchen	Manshun
Nitrate	Recital	Justify
Bullion	Chansellor	Varity

4.

Amalgamation	Technician	Obsession
Geneology	Journul	Knife
Magazine	Humility	Radiate

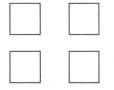

5.

Zylophone	Penicillin	Orcastra
Pantomime	Parocail	Utility
Ceremonious	Anaesthesia	Omission

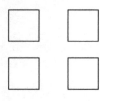

6.

Warranty	League	Appesement
Divercity	Guillotine	Scientist
Tanjible	Temporarily	Latitute

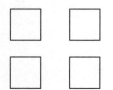

7.

Hereditable	Indentation	Resital
Frustrate	Dismantel	Arbitary
Omission	Rondevous	Nominate

8.

Ridiculuous	Scraach	Expedient
Segregate	Numeration	Petition
Quinine	Satallite	League

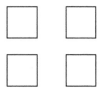

9.

Quadangle	Solemize	Lagging
Rapture	Obsesion	Nitrate
Alternate	Undulate	Warrantee

10.

Nutritious	Rapchure	Welthiness
Hereditable	Indentation	Latitude
Scaffolding	Flippant	Temprarily

END OF EXERCISE

10.   Reading for information

You are presented with some passages to read. A number of statements follow each passage. Your task is to say whether the statement
is true or false. The statement can only be true if the information in the
passage bears this out.

Example:
The great fire of London started in Pudding Lane, near London
Bridge, in the year 1666. It was probably the worst fire in the City's
history.

1.   The great fire of London took place in 1666.

     <u>True</u> or False (underline one of these)

When the American War of Independence started, the Americans
had no regular army. But one was soon formed under the
command of George Washington. However, this army was badly
equipped and lacked proper training.

The war lasted for six years, from 1775 to 1781, and the
Americans drew up the formal Declaration of Independence on 4
July 1776. This stated that the United States would be an inde-
pendent republic.

1.   The highly trained American army quickly won the war.

     True or False

2.   The war lasted for six years and the Declaration of Independence
     was made shortly after the end of the war.

     True or False

3.   The first regular American army was commanded by
     Washington.

     True or False

The brain begins to show signs of decline after a certain proportion of the nerve cells of which it is formed have died. As people get older they have fewer and fewer nerve cells, because once the cells have died they are not replaced.

By the time a person reaches the age of 75 as many as a quarter of the nerve cells may have died.

Although science has advanced a great deal and scientists today are better placed to study how our brain functions, there is still a great deal to discover.

4. By the time a person is in his mid-seventies he may have lost as many as 25 per cent of his nerve cells.

    True or False

5. Scientists today are able to cure the dying nerve cells, because of the great advances made by science.

    True or False

6. The brain cells, like the skin cells, are able to multiply and that is why all the brain cells do not die out.

    True or False

The problem with the notion of technology is that there are various meanings of the term. It no longer has a precise and limited meaning, but rather a vague and expansive one.

The term is used to describe not only instruments and machines but also skills, methods and procedures, among other things.

Some commentators have argued that technology is a factor that determines key facets of organisations.

However, others have argued that there is no cause and effect relationship between adoption of the technologies and the structural and performance outcomes that may be associated with them.

7.   Everyone agrees with the single definition of technology.

     True or False

8.   When people talk about technology they are always referring to machines, such as computers.

     True or False

9.   Some people have argued that technology is a determining factor in a number of key areas of an organisation.

     True or False

For more (and more difficult) examples of this type of question, see *How to Pass Graduate Psychometric Tests* (published by Kogan Page).

A different style of reading for information question

In the following questions you are given a series of passages each of which is followed by a number of statements. It is your task to say whether the statement is true or false or whether it is not possible to say if the statement is true or false. You should base your decision only on the information or opinions given in the passage.

You should judge the statement to be true only if, for example, it follows logically from the passage or is a rewording of something contained in the statement or is a valid summary of the statement or a part of it.

You should judge the statement to be false if it, for example, cannot follow logically from the statement or if it contradicts something contained in the passage.

If you require further information than is contained in the passage before you can tell if the statement is true or false then you should record your answer as cannot tell.

Passage 1

Our solar system has nine planets, each of which orbits the sun in an anticlockwise direction on the same plane so forming a disc-shaped system. The four inner ones, Mercury, Venus, Earth and Mars, are spheres of rock while the four much larger outer planets, Jupiter, Saturn, Uranus and Neptune, are gigantic balls of gas with liquid and solid cores. Pluto is the exception in that it is the most distant of the planets from the sun but is, like the inner planets, made up of a sphere of rock rather than a large amount of gas, as are its distant neighbours. All the outer planets and two of the inner planets have at least one moon. Saturn has the most with 20.

Q1   Mercury is the planet closest to the sun.
        True
        False
        Cannot tell

                                  Answer box

Q2   Pluto has at least one moon.
        True
        False
        Cannot tell

                                  Answer box

Q3   There are four outer planets.
      True
      False
      Cannot tell

                          Answer box

      [   ]

Q4   Mars is further from the sun than Jupiter.
      True
      False
      Cannot tell

                          Answer box

      [   ]

Passage 2
High blood pressure or hypertension is caused by poor diet, drinking too much alcohol and obesity. It can be reduced by losing weight, improving one's diet, taking exercise and drinking moderate amounts of alcohol. Hypertension is believed to be the single most common contributor to early death in adults worldwide as it causes heart and kidney disease. It is estimated that 1 billion people suffer from high blood pressure and that the number of sufferers is forecast to increase further still both in developed and developing countries.

Q5   The incidence of high blood pressure is on the rise around the world.
     True
     False
     Cannot tell

                              Answer box

     ┌─────────────────────────────────┐
     │   │
     │   │
     └─────────────────────────────────┘

Q6   One billion people will die worldwide from high blood pressure.
     True
     False
     Cannot tell

                              Answer box

     ┌─────────────────────────────────┐
     │   │
     │   │
     └─────────────────────────────────┘

Q7   Hypertension is irreversible.
     True
     False
     Cannot tell

                              Answer box

     ┌─────────────────────────────────┐
     │   │
     │   │
     └─────────────────────────────────┘

Q8   The rise in cases of high blood pressure will be more marked in developed countries.
True
False
Cannot tell

Answer box

Passage 3
In some parts of the world the interval between high water or high tide is one day while in other parts of the world there are two high tides every 24 hours. The difference in height between high and low water varies greatly depending on the location. In some places the range can be almost 10 metres, while other places experience a range between high and low water of only approximately a metre or less. These tides are caused by gravitational and centrifugal force. Despite the sun's immense mass it is the much closer moon that provides twice the sun's gravitational pull on the world's oceans. This lunar force causes the water to be drawn to the side of the Earth facing the moon. On the opposite side to the moon a second bulge of water occurs caused by the centrifugal force created by the spin of both the Earth and the moon. It is these bulges of water that are the high tides.

Q9   The gravitation pull of the sun does not affect the world's oceans.
True
False
Cannot tell

Answer box

Q10 The location where the interval between high and low water is one day also experiences the greatest range between high and low water.
True
False
Cannot tell

Answer box

Q11 The gravitational pull of moons of Saturn also affects the world's oceans.
True
False
Cannot tell

Answer box

Q12 The passage states that centrifugal force causes the ocean to bulge.
True
False
Cannot tell

Answer box

Passage 4

The medieval period lasted from 1000 to 1500. It was preceded by the Dark Ages. Many towns were formed across Europe during this period as trade and populations increased. Kings ruled and with the leaders of the church they decided state affairs. Most people lived in the countryside and worked on the land. They gave a share of their produce to the local lord in return for protection and as rent. They had to work very hard and for much of their lives lived in abject poverty. Life expectancy for the commoner was much shorter than it is today. As a result of the expansion of trade coins became commonplace.

Q13 The medieval period lasted for 500 years.
      True
      False
      Cannot tell

                              Answer box

      ┌─────────────────────────────────────┐
      │   │
      │   │
      └─────────────────────────────────────┘

Q14 The majority of the population lived in the countryside.
      True
      False
      Cannot tell

                              Answer box

      ┌─────────────────────────────────────┐
      │   │
      │   │
      └─────────────────────────────────────┘

Q15 When a harvest failed or was poor the commoner risked star-
vation.
True
False
Cannot tell

Answer box

Q16 The Dark Ages followed the medieval period.
True
False
Cannot tell

Answer box

Passage 5
Radio waves are a type of energy and create electromagnetic fields.
They form part of the electromagnetic spectrum, which includes
visible light, microwaves and x rays. We are exposed to many electromagnetic forces, for example when we turn on a light or television.
These forces have a heating effect, which is used in a microwave oven
to heat food. Mobile phones work by transmitting and receiving radio
waves and because the phone is held close to our heads it is suggested
that the heating effect might cause harm to our brains.

Q17 The passage states that emissions from mobile phones could warm brain tissue.
True
False
Cannot tell

Answer box

Q18 Mobile phones create electromagnetic fields.
True
False
Cannot tell

Answer box

Q19 Radio waves are a part of the electromagnetic spectrum.
True
False
Cannot tell

Answer box

Q20 Children are especially vulnerable because they have thinner
     skulls and a developing nervous system.
     True
     False
     Cannot tell

                              Answer box

     ┌─────────────────────────────────────┐
     │   │
     │   │
     └─────────────────────────────────────┘

Passage 6
A study in the 1960s followed up in their adult life 800 children who
had achieved in psychometric tests of ability scores in the top 1% for
their age group. It was reported that 90% of this population had
entered university and that 70% had graduated. The study found that
the group of adults between them had written 70 books and almost
1000 scientific papers. Some, however, had served prison sentences,
while others reported unhappy careers and marriages. A second study
followed up on very low scoring children. It was found that most
when retested as adults obtained scores that were average. A far lower
percentage of the low scoring children had gone to university and
more reported unhappy careers. The rate for criminal conviction and
the incidence of adult mental health problems were reported to be
broadly similar across the two groups.

Q21 Long-term forecasts made from childhood scores in psycho-
     metric tests are not very accurate.
     True
     False
     Cannot tell

                              Answer box

     ┌─────────────────────────────────────┐
     │   │
     │   │
     └─────────────────────────────────────┘

Q22 The passage states that the grades realised at university corre-
lated well with the childhood test scores.
True
False
Cannot tell

Answer box

Q23 The passage suggests that many of the low scoring children as
adults had greatly improved their performance in the tests.
True
False
Cannot tell

Answer box

Q24 Most of the differences between these groups in terms of perfor-
mance in the test and success in work as adults can be attributed
to the amount and quality of education received.
True
False
Cannot tell

Answer box

Passage 7

The world's population is determined by the balance between the birth rate and the death rate. The population of a particular area can also increase or decrease due to migration. It will increase when the number of immigrants exceeds the number of emigrants and decrease when the number of emigrants exceeds the number of immigrants. The make-up of a population by its age and sex and its life-expectancy will also have implications for the population size and its expected future growth or decline.

Q25 The world's population overall will not be affected by immigration or emigration.
   True
   False
   Cannot tell

Answer box

Q26 A higher birth rate will mean a growing world population.
   True
   False
   Cannot tell

Answer box

Q27 The world's population will continue to grow.
     True
     False
     Cannot tell

                              Answer box

Q28 The population of a particular area will decrease if the number
     of immigrants is higher than the number of emigrants.
     True
     False
     Cannot tell

                              Answer box

Passage 8
The United States of America is the fourth largest country in the
world, the third most populated and the wealthiest. It is made up of 50
states, 48 of which occupy the central part of the North American
continent. Its population of 280 million is multiracial as a result of
waves of immigrants arriving from Europe, Africa, Asia and South
America. Its wealth is derived from its industrial output, its world-
leading technologies and science, its extensive agriculture and forestry
and vast natural resources including oil, coal and metal ores. It is estimated that something like 45 million tourists visit America each year,
which makes tourism another very important contributor to the
American economy.

Q29 The passage states that the main languages spoken in America are English and Spanish.
True
False
Cannot tell

Answer box

Q30 Its vast industrial output has made America the wealthiest nation on earth.
True
False
Cannot tell

Answer box

Q31 The currency used in America is the US dollar.
True
False
Cannot tell

Answer box

Q32 The world's fourth most populous nation has a population of less than 281 million.
True
False
Cannot tell

Answer box

Passage 9
The Azores are just one of several island groups that are spread across the Atlantic Ocean. To the south lie Madeira and the Canary Islands, the Cape Verde Islands and further south still the Ascension and St Helena. Madeira and the Canary Islands are developed holiday destinations visited by tens of thousands of visitors each year. The Cape Verde Islands and the islands further south are much quieter with no sprawling holiday resorts, only traditional villages, giving the visitor the chance to explore remote island life. All the islands share a volcanic geology and have spectacular volcanic coastlines and interiors. Unique and sometimes rare flora and fauna are found on them all.

Q33 The Azores group are found to the north of the Canaries.
True
False
Cannot tell

Answer box

Q34 The Azores are a developed holiday destination like Madeira with sprawling holiday resorts.
True
False
Cannot tell

Answer box

Q35 The Cape Verde Islands are south of St Helena.
True
False
Cannot tell

Answer box

Q36 Remote island life can be experienced on Ascension.
True
False
Cannot tell

Answer box

Passage 10

Some years ago the Government tried to put into practice the principle that fines for criminal offences should be linked to the income of the offender. People found guilty of a crime had to indicate to which income bracket they belonged and this was used to decide the level of the fine. After a few months the Government withdrew the initiative because it produced some decisions that struck the general public as very unfair. For example, people on very high earnings were fined many thousands of pounds for minor offences while those with no income were fined only a few pounds for some really quite serious crimes. Commentators concluded that the public prefer a system where a fine acts as a deterrent and for this to happen the person fined should to some extent struggle to pay it but at the same time a fine should be proportionate to the seriousness of the offence.

Q37 A fine of £200 is proportionate to the offence of dropping litter but would be a greater deterrent to someone with a modest income than someone who is rich.
True
False
Cannot tell

Answer box

Q38 The public prefer a system where the rich are fined thousands of pounds for minor offences.
True
False
Cannot tell

Answer box

Q39 Under the old system it was possible that two offenders found guilty of the same offence for which they were equally to blame were fined the same amount.
True
False
Cannot tell

Answer box

Q40 The public no longer hold that fines should bear some relationship to the income of offenders.
True
False
Cannot tell

Answer box

11.   Alphabetical order

The alphabet: A B C D E F G H I J K L M N O P Q R S T U V W X Y Z

Arranging words – Example 1

Place the following words in the answer box in alphabetical order:

Gangster	Kidnap
Puff-adder	Sorrow
Acrobat	Orator
Heiress	Reptile

Answer

1.	5.
2.	6.
3.	7.
4.	8.

Arranging words – Example 2

Now arrange the following into alphabetical order:

Faithful	Foliage
Fixer	Farmyard
Florida	Fabric
February	Feather

Answer

1.	5.
2.	6.
3.	7.
4.	8.

Rearranging letters

1. Rearrange the letters in 'charity' into alphabetical order. Place your answer in the answer box.

Answer box

2. Rearrange the letters in 'liquor' into alphabetical order. Place your answer in the answer box.

Answer box

3. Rearrange the letters in 'organic' into alphabetical order. Place your answer in the answer box.

Answer box

4. Rearrange the letters in 'Thames' into alphabetical order. Place your answer in the answer box.

Answer box

5. Take the letters that occur in 'Delphi' but not in 'delta' and write them in alphabetical order in the answer box.

Answer box

6. Take the letters that occur in 'kidney' but not in 'kilograms' and write them in alphabetical order in the answer box.

Answer box

7. Take the letters that occur in 'petrol' but not in 'Peru' and write them in alphabetical order in the answer box.

Answer box

8. Take the letters that occur in 'chamber' but not in 'chaise' and write them in alphabetical order in the answer box.

Answer box

Over the page you will find a timed exercise that requires knowledge of alphabetical order.

Before you turn over, set a clock or watch and allow yourself **three** minutes.

Timed exercise

Instructions

Alongside each name write the file number under which the name should be placed.

The first two examples have been completed.

File numbers

1.	A–Am	10.	J–K
2.	An–Az	11.	L–M
3.	B–Bs	12.	N–O
4.	Bt–Bz	13.	P–Q
5.	C–Ck	14.	R
6.	Cl–Cz	15.	S
7.	D–E	16.	T
8.	F–G	17.	U–V
9.	H–I	18.	W–X,Y–Z

Name	File Number	Name	File Number
Young	18	Warner	_____
Bayard	3	Carrington	_____
Harvey	_____	Christie	_____
Fisher	_____	Tooling	_____
Skinner	_____	Arnold	_____
Bishop	_____	Hood	_____
Adler	_____	Dell	_____

12.   Comparisons 1

1.   Man is to boy as woman is to:

   A. Lady   B. Girl   C. Madam   D. Lad

2.   Food is to eat as water is to:

   A. Swallow B. Bathe   C. Drink   D. Shower

3.   Man is to house as monkey is to:

   A. Tree   B. Jungle   C. Cave   D. Nest

4.   Car is to bicycle as aeroplane is to:

   A. Jet   B. Sky   C. Glider   D. Flying

5.   Ship is to sea as train is to:

   A. Station   B. Platform   C. Rail   D. Journey

6.   He is to him as she is to:

   A. She's   B. Her   C. Their   D. Hers

7.   Cotton is to thread as copper is to:

   A. Mesh   B. Wire   C. Electricity   D. Insulation

8.   Shoes are to feet as gloves are to:

   A. Fingers B. Hands   C. Toes   D. Arms

9.   Hat is to head as sweater is to:

   A. Chest   B. Torso   C. Arms   D. Back

10. Floppy disk is to computer as a suitcase is to:

   A. Teacher B. Traveller   C. Technician   D. Trainee

Comparisons 2

Now try the following and see how many you can do in **two** minutes.

1. Pen is to ink as pencil is to:

    A. Quill   B. Lead   C. Eraser   D. Crayon

2. Black is to white as light is to:

    A. Lamp   B. Bulb   C. Dark   D. Bright

3. A is to B as Y is to:

    A. Z   B. Y   C. X   D. W

4. M is to P as G is to:

    A. H   B. L   C. J   D. N

5. F is to L as R is to:

    A. X   B. Y   C. H   D. G

6. Eraser is to pencil as snowpake is to:

    A. Chalk   B. Pen   C. Paintbrush   D. Stencil

7. Story book is to read as exercise book is to:

    A. Study   B. Doodle   C. Write   D. Draw

13.   Odd-one-out

1. A. Computer   B. Printer   C. Mouse   D. Keyboard   E. Monitor
2. A. Hands   B. Feet   C. Fingers   D. Brain   E. Eyes
3. A. See   B. Taste   C. Hear   D. Nose   E. Feel
4. A. Wrist   B. Elbow   C. Finger   D. Thumb   E. Toe
5. A. Dry   B. Arid   C. Parched   D. Desert   E. Swamp
6. A. Horse   B. Camel   C. Pig   D. Oxen   E. Elephant
7. A. Pen   B. Pencil   C. Quill   D. Chalk   E. Stencil
8. A. Lion   B. Tiger   C. Leopard   D. Baboon   E. Cheetah
9. A. Lantern   B. Lamp   C. Sun   D. Candle   E. Torch
10. A. Lake   B. Pond   C. River   D. Reservoir   E. Pool
11. A. Telephone   B. Television   C. Facsimile   D. Telex   E. E-mail
12. A. Teacher   B. Trainer   C. Lecturer   D. Instructor   E. Examiner

14.   Opposites

1. Down is the opposite of:
   A. Horizontal   B. Up   C. Fallen   D. Crouching

2. Inflated is the opposite of:
   A. Blown-up   B. Deflated   C. Reflated   D. Conflated

3. Append is the opposite of:
   A. Add   B. Restore   C. Remove   D. Revert

4. Correct is the opposite of:
   A. Solution   B. Error   C. Right   D. True

5. Enter is the opposite of:
   A. Come in   B. Arrive   C. Exit   D. Welcome

6. Covert is the opposite of:
   A. Closed   B. Open   C. Divert   D. Revert

7. Restore is the opposite of:
   A. Destroy   B. Repair   C. Reinstate   D. Mend

8. Drunk is the opposite of:

   A. Tipsy   B. Sober   C. Intoxicated   D. Incapable

9. Cool is the opposite of:

   A. Freeze   B. Warm   C. Boil   D. Frozen

10. Vertical is the opposite of:

    A. Upright   B. Erect   C. Horizontal   D. Upside-down

15. Similar sounding words but different spelling and meanings

In this exercise you have to find a word that sounds the same as the word that you are given but is spelt differently.

Exercise 1
For example:

full   *fool*

1.	Sight _____	2.	Course _____
3.	Draft _____	4.	Broach _____
5.	New _____	6.	Dam _____
7.	Weather _____	8.	Due _____
9.	Mail _____	10.	Die _____
11.	Gale _____	12.	Sweet _____
13.	Write _____	14.	To _____
15.	Read _____	16.	Tail _____
17.	Bye _____	18.	One _____
19.	Wave _____	20.	For _____
21.	Need _____	22.	Flower _____
23.	Breach _____	24.	Sole _____
25.	Seen _____	26.	Hair _____
27.	Sun _____	28.	Heard _____
29.	Seem _____	30.	Heart _____

Exercise 2
See how many you can do in **five** minutes.

1.	Fate	_____	2.	Hear	_____
3.	Great	_____	4.	Hole	_____
5.	No	_____	6.	Main	_____
7.	Bored	_____	8.	Ale	_____
9.	Bold	_____	10.	Night	_____
11.	Bare	_____	12.	Knit	_____
13.	Brake	_____	14.	Miner	_____
15.	Bread	_____	16.	Naval	_____
17.	Sent	_____	18.	None	_____
19.	Meet	_____	20.	Or	_____
21.	Of	_____	22.	Peace	_____
23.	Peel	_____	24.	Pair	_____
25.	Peek	_____	26.	Plate	_____
27.	Pole	_____	28.	Pull	_____
29.	Pour	_____	30.	Rain	_____
31.	Pray	_____	32.	Program	_____
33.	Pearl	_____	34.	Key	_____
35.	Rest	_____	36.	Rap	_____
37.	Reek	_____	38.	Ring	_____
39.	Rye	_____	40.	Shoe	_____

16.   Written statements/tests

Sometimes when you attend an interview you are asked to write a short statement, of at least 50 words, explaining why you want the job or what you think are the most important aspects of the work. A time limit is imposed.

You are usually told in advance that you will be asked to undertake such an exercise so you can prepare your statement beforehand.

If you know that you are going to have to write a statement, ask someone to help you prepare it. If you keep the sentences short your statement will be easier to read.

Make sure your statement is positive. Consider incorporating, in your own words, points about the work made in the advertisement or information sent to you by the organisation.

You should memorise your statement the night before. Read it aloud again and again, then write it out repeatedly. Keep learning your statement until you are able to write it without notes or prompting. Learn the spelling of any words of which you are unsure.

Try writing your statement in the time that you are allowed – usually 10 minutes – and make sure that your handwriting is neat and legible.

17.   Homophones

These are words that sound the same but are spelt differently and have a different meaning.

In this exercise you are presented with a list of words. You are required to find another word that sounds the same but is spelt differently and has a different meaning.

You should try to do these in less than **three** minutes.

1. Him   _____
2. Sight   _____
3. Bold   _____
4. Seem   _____
5. Been   _____
6. Ring   _____
7. Right   _____
8. Night   _____
9. Fought   _____
10. Threw   _____
11. Bow   _____
12. Rung   _____
13. Pain   _____

14. Wait   _____
15. Brake   _____
16. Great   _____
17. New   _____
18. No   _____
19. See   _____
20. Where   _____

18.   More homophones

In this exercise you are again presented with a list of words. You are required to find another word that sounds the same but is spelt differently and has a different meaning.

1. Here   _____
2. Bare   _____
3. Fair   _____
4. Hair   _____
5. Tea   _____
6. Pear   _____
7. Dear   _____
8. For   _____
9. Bate   _____
10. Fate   _____
11. Bale   _____
12. Sale   _____
13. Ale   _____
14. Tale   _____
15. Vale   _____
16. Whale   _____
17. Which   _____

18. Pale   _____
19. War   _____
20. Sun   _____

19.   Homophones again

In this exercise you are presented with a list of words again. You are required to find another word that sounds the same but is spelt differently and has a different meaning.

1. Male   _____
2. Two   _____
3. Sew   _____
4. Hole   _____
5. Flare   _____
6. Dough   _____
7. Key   _____
8. Plain   _____
9. Check   _____
10. Fur   _____
11. Not   _____
12. Queue   _____
13. Leak   _____
14. Feet   _____
15. Beat   _____
16. Bore   _____
17. Bored   _____
18. You   _____
19. Sweet   _____
20. Tire   _____

20.   Synonyms

These are words that are spelt differently and sound different but have similar meanings

In this exercise you are required to match words that have similar meanings, from column 1 with those in column 2. In column 3 you should write the word from column 1 that has the similar meaning with the word in column 2.

Try these and see if you can do them in less than **three** minutes

The first one has been done for you!

	Column 1	Column 2	Column 3
1	Fight	Nearby	Close
2	Sea	Climb	
3	Friend	Absolute	
4	Enemy	Foreign	
5	Far	Abuse	
6	Concept	Distant	
7	Abduct	Ocean	
8	Complete	Arbiter	
9	Misuse	Mate	
10	Alien	Aroma	
11	Similar	Brawl	
12	Judge	Foe	
13	Fragrance	Idea	
14	Ascend	Kidnap	
15	Close	Alike	
16	Audio	Behind	
17	Bandit	Benefit	
18	Rear	Garbage	
19	Advantage	Outlaw	
20	Rubbish	Sound	

21.   More synonyms

In the following exercises you are again required to match words that have similar meanings, from column 1 with those in column 2. In column 3 you should write the word from column 1 that has the similar meaning with the word in column 2.

	Column 1	Column 2	Column 3
1	Garbage	Empty	
2	Gaol	Wound	
3	Blank	Least	
4	Latrine	Grab	
5	Present	Channel	
6	Close	Insect	
7	Fleer	Refuse	
8	Gash	Jail	
9	Smallest	Sham	
10	Seize	Drum	
11	Groove	Border	
12	Bug	Pester	
13	Bogus	Fragile	
14	Counter	Inferior	
15	Curd	Lavatory	
16	Crummy	Oppose	
17	Brittle	Sneer	
18	Bother	Shut	
19	Boundary	Gift	
20	Bongo	Cheese	

	Column 1	Column 2	Column 3
1	Mad	Rude	
2	Odour	Sailor	
3	Moisture	Foe	
4	Prohibit	Unite	
5	Broad	Fable	
6	Curb	Sharp	
7	Coarse	Weariness	
8	Conceal	Feeble	
9	Interior	Round	
10	Difficult	Dwelling	
11	Insolent	Insane	
12	Join	Smell	
13	Mariner	Dampness	
14	Enemy	Forbid	
15	Myth	Wide	
16	Acute	Control	
17	Fatigue	Rough	
18	Weak	Hide	
19	Circular	Inside	
20	Abode	Hard	

	Column 1	Column 2	Column 3
1	Buy	Peaceful	
2	Rank	Clear	
3	Rapid	Riches	
4	Remedy	Strict	
5	Reveal	Horse	
6	Sturdy	Slim	
7	Surrender	Position	
8	Sleek	Empty	
9	Suspend	Annually	
10	Tranquil	Defeat	
11	Steed	Anger	
12	Slender	Quick	
13	Futile	Purchase	
14	Vacant	Pointless	
15	Yearly	Cure	
16	Vanquish	Show	
17	Stern	Strong	
18	Wealth	Yield	
19	Wrath	Smooth	
20	Transparent	Hang	

22.   Antonyms

These are words that have opposite meanings.

In this exercise you are required to find the word that has an opposite meaning from the box below and match it with the word in the list.

1. Opponent	8. Low	15. Rear
2. Hard	9. Liquid	16. Below
3. Bright	10. Good	17. Open
4. Dull	11. Evil	18. Shut
5. Foe	12. Front	19. Friend
6. Rigid	13. Closed	20. Tight
7. Bendable	14. Right	

1.   Flexible   [   ]   Answer

2.   Solid   [   ]   Answer

3.   Shiny   [   ]   Answer

4.   Enemy   [   ]   Answer

5   High   [   ]   Answer

6.   Above   [   ]   Answer

7.   Back   [   ]   Answer

8.   Left   [   ]   Answer

9.   Shut   [   ]   Answer

10. Bad   [   ]   Answer

23.   More antonyms

In this exercise you are again required to find the word that has an opposite meaning from the box below and match it with the word in the list.

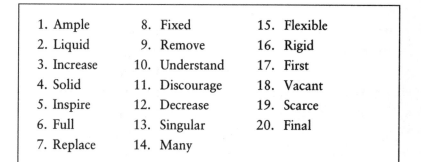

1. Ample	8. Fixed	15. Flexible
2. Liquid	9. Remove	16. Rigid
3. Increase	10. Understand	17. First
4. Solid	11. Discourage	18. Vacant
5. Inspire	12. Decrease	19. Scarce
6. Full	13. Singular	20. Final
7. Replace	14. Many	

1.   Empty   Answer

2.   Last   Answer

3.   Fluid   Answer

4.   Increment   Answer

5.   Loose   Answer

6.   Motivate   Answer

7.   Extract   Answer

8.   Plural   Answer

9.   Pliable   Answer

10. Plenty   Answer

24.   Creating compound words

In this exercise you are required to select two words from each row to create a new single word (a compound word).

For example: the words SUN and DAY can be combined to create a new single word SUNDAY.

See how many you can do in **five** minutes – time your self accurately. Underline the two words that you think can form a new single word.

1	Sun	Moon	Day	Year	Pluto
2	He	She	Her	Art	Design
3	Motor	Train	Lorry	Car	Plane
4	Flip	Turn	Side	Arm	Mat
5	Even	After	Affray	Affirm	Noon
6	Allow	True	Able	Alpha	Alpine
7	Alpha	Race	Bet	Alms	Also
8	Amalgam	Alter	Always	Never	Ate
9	Anti	Month	Body	Hand	Leg
10	God	Anti	Heaven	Christ	Saint
11	Anti	Day	Month	Social	Year
12	Hear	Audio	Listen	Meter	Here
13	Car	Auto	Draw	Graph	Authority
14	Auto	Bend	Turn	Friend	Mate
15	Front	Back	Top	Hand	Toe
16	Back	Clock	Watch	Ache	Round
17	Desk	Back	Chair	Ward	Book
18	Bag	Scale	Pipe	Exercise	Hard
19	High	Height	Land	Ocean	Black
20	Lorry	Rail	Trail	Way	Freight
21	Base	Case	Fall	Ball	Tall
22	Bat	Cat	Ten	Seven	Ben
23	Do	Be	Never	Come	Proper
24	Bed	Chair	Dress	Clothes	Shoes
25	Pot	Bed	Hat	Pat	Pan

25.   More compound words

In this exercise you are again required to select two words from each line to create a new single word (a compound word).

See how many you can do in **five** minutes. Underline the two words that you think can form a new single word.

1	Blind	Deaf	Day	Month	Date
2	Pot	Pan	Block	Hard	Age
3	Brother	Bother	All	Some	Sister
4	Top	Bottom	Under	More	Less
5	Foot	Hole	Blind	Sport	Spot
6	Flour	Bread	Butter	Crumb	Cheese
7	Slow	Broke	Break	Speed	Fast
8	Table	Blind	Beauty	Task	Fold
9	Bride	Woman	Man	Groom	Father
10	Brief	Face	Base	Case	Lace
11	Brunt	Brute	Fine	Back	Force
12	Break	Quick	Able	Speedily	Hard
13	Beads	Chain	Round	Saw	Seen
14	Sit	Chair	Table	Boy	Man
15	Chamber	Sleep	House	Maid	Paid
16	Grooms	Brides	Butler	Maid	Servant
17	Yellow	Colour	Full	Blind	Tense
18	Common	Sensor	Fever	Wealth	Poverty
19	Copy	Work	Right	Sight	Letter
20	Wheat	Corn	Solidly	Wall	Lightly
21	Counter	Shelf	Soil	Foil	Boil
22	Fall	Crash	Tumble	Over	Land
23	Charter	Scale	Counter	Taste	Balance
24	Band	Counter	Sand	Act	Display
25	Centre	Push	Table	Chair	Spoon

26.   Compound words again

Try this exercise again. See how many you can do in **five** minutes.
Underline the two words that you think can form a new single word.

1	Arms	Coat	Pattern	Hanger	Banger
2	Gear	Motor	Cane	Stick	Bus
3	Import	Export	Insect	Ant	Bee
4	Abroad	Home	Officer	Work	Factory
5	Honey	Sugar	Brush	Comb	Sweet
6	Hour	Day	Plastic	Glass	Paper
7	Male	Man	Female	Rude	Kind
8	Alive	Dead	String	Line	Foot
9	Snow	Ice	Milk	Cream	Butter
10	Sun	Honey	Earth	Sweeter	Moon
11	Honey	Lot	Dot	Pot	Bread
12	Bed	Fed	Like	Linen	Led
13	Beet	Beat	Foot	Cook	Root
14	Be	Root	Hold	Bold	Sold
15	Birth	Death	Year	Month	Day
16	White	Black	Toe	Head	Mouth
17	Church	Temple	Warden	Police	Guest
18	School	Class	More	Less	Greater
19	Cloak	Tower	Person	Room	Tier
20	Simple	Grand	People	Fun	Father
21	Coast	Sea	Boat	Guard	Soldier
22	Hat	Fat	Him	Her	Them
23	Game	Sport	Keeper	Find	Giver
24	Flat	Plat	Born	Form	From
25	Cat	Sat	Pot	Urn	Ten

27.   Four-minute compound words

See how many you can do in **four** minutes. Underline the two words
that you think can form a new single word.

1	Bread	Broad	Cost	Cast	Frost
2	Brother	Uncle	Hood	Rude	Food
3	Thump	Bump	Sister	Father	Kin
4	Bus	Train	Queen	King	Lorry
5	Tap	Cap	Rat	Able	Kane
6	Care	Mare	More	Less	Great
7	Car	Van	Pot	Rot	Got
8	Check	Pit	Bore	Mate	Rate
9	Waste	Cart	Car	Pound	Ton
10	Thin	Wide	Broad	Road	Way
11	Common	Rare	Site	Place	Distance
12	Complain	Disagree	Pest	Bug	Ant
13	Rough	Gentle	Ghost	Man	Train
14	Ticket	Gate	Lost	Kiosk	Way
15	For	Four	Given	Taken	Miss
16	Bear	Fox	Rodent	Hound	Terrier
17	Fond	Taste	Ant	Hate	Twist
18	Dream	Hear	Foot	Hurt	Steps
19	Eye	Nose	Hair	Brow	Brown
20	Feat	Them	Her	Escape	Hands
21	Cloth	Fabric	Tempt	Ate	Past
22	Mate	Friend	Boat	Liner	Ship
23	Foot	Leg	Sky	Path	Ground
24	Sport	Game	Play	Ball	Keeper
25	Cool	Warm	Ant	Freeze	Spider

28.   Three-minute compound words

See how many you can do in **three** minutes. Underline the two words
that you think can form a new single word.

1	Fruit	Vegetable	Greater	Less	Given
2	Lost	Gain	Half	Fully	Empty
3	Doctor	For	Against	Ward	Board
4	Four	Number	Lots	Some	Many
5	Frame	Around	Work	Idol	Hardly
6	Estate	Land	Guard	Train	Mark
7	Eye	Face	Pan	Cook	Lid
8	Travel	Fare	Country	Home	Well
9	Cot	Bed	Weight	Pound	Ton
10	Front	Feed	Male	Person	Back
11	For	Against	Play	Tune	Sing
12	Grate	Gate	Door	Crash	Accident
13	Plane	Fly	Bug	Wheel	Under
14	God	Heaven	Boy	Hell	Son
15	Against	For	Young	Age	Male
16	Dark	Day	Flash	Front	Back
17	Dart	Arrow	Mouth	Face	Spear
18	Body	Eye	Wet	Sight	Truth
19	Under	Over	Metal	Mine	Your
20	Count	Numbers	Many	Less	Over
21	Good	Kind	Estate	Will	Lord
22	Large	Grand	Run	Sit	Stand
23	Plane	Fly	Twist	Over	Truth
24	Post	Counter	Holder	Part	Spares
25	Foot	Twister	Hold	Break	Gone

29.   Analogies

1. Cat is to mouse as spider is to:
   (a) web   (b) fly   (c) scorpion   (d) bathroom

2. Cat is to kitten as dog is to:
   (a) canine   (b) labrador   (c) pup   (d) Fido

3. One is to single as two is to:
   (a) many   (b) three   (c) more   (d) couple

4. Wing is to bird as fin is to:
   (a) duck   (b) fish   (c) heron   (d) flamingo

5. Father is to son as mother is to:
   (a) daughter   (b) sibling   (c) female   (d) women

6. January is to February as November is to:
   (a) October   (b) December   (c) September   (d) August

7. Shell is to egg as rind is to:
   (a) apple   (b) pear   (c) orange   (d) cherry

8. Water is to pipes as electricity is to:
   (a) generators   (b) pylons   (c) wires   (d) switch

9. Tree is to forest as sheep is to:
   (a) herd   (b) gaggle   (c) pack   (d) flock

10. Left is to right as west is to:
    (a) east   (b) west   (c) north   (d) south

11. Early is to late as stop is to:
    (a) halt   (b) commence   (c) refrain   (d) complete

12. Centimetres is to metre as inches is to:

    (a) foot   (b) yard   (c) fathom   (d) mile

13. Radio is to listen as book is to:

    (a) look   (b) peruse   (c) encode   (d) comprehensive

14. Vicar is to church as curator is to:

    (a) museum   (b) school   (c) temple   (d) station

15. Pilot is to aeroplane as driver is to:

    (a) automobile   (b) spaceship   (c) ship   (d) horse

16. Elephant is to herd as lion is to:

    (a) flock   (b) pack   (c) herd   (d) pride

17. Wolf is to pack as locust is to:

    (a) herd   (b) plague   (c) bevy   (d) crew

18. Cattle is to herd as monkey is to:

    (a) team   (b) tribe   (c) troop   (d) gang

19. Bird is to flock as whale is to:

    (a) school   (b) shoal   (c) band   (d) gang

20. Sailor is to crew as dancer is to:

    (a) gaggle   (b) troupe   (c) host   (d) choir

21. Tree is to forest as book is to:

    (a) shelf   (b) reader   (c) library   (d) pulp

22. Banana is to bunch as leopard is to:

    (a) pride   (b) leap   (c) nest   (d) pace

23. Audience is to concert as congregation is to:

(a) riot   (b) street   (c) mass   (d) football match

24. Dozen is to 12 as couple is to:

(a) one   (b) two   (c) three   (d) four

25. Cat is to kitten as eel is to:

(a) eel   (b) eeler   (c) elver   (d) elder

Numerical tests

On pages 122–53 you will find practice examples, which you can work through at your own pace and which become progressively harder. You will also find timed examples. We have tried to ensure that the severity of these timed examples is comparable to the types of question you would face in a real selection test.

If you can do the timed sums, or learn to do them, in the time suggested, you can have confidence in yourself because you are likely to do well in most types of numerical test.

Do not use a calculator except to check your answers. There is not space here to show you how to do these calculations. If you are unable to do some of them, ask a friend to show you. Alternatively, your local library will have books that demonstrate how to do these sums together with further practice examples.

Some tests set out to measure your skills in approximating the answer to calculations. Even if you do not have to face such a test, it is a useful skill to develop as it can lead to your being far quicker in many types of numerical test, and can also help to keep a check on calculations performed on a calculator.

To help you develop this skill we have provided you with estimating exercises for each of the four rules and for fractions and percentages. Estimating is very useful in the case of multiple-choice numerical tests.

When you approximate, do not work the sum out; instead, use your knowledge of the relationship between numbers to make an educated guess at the answer. Round up numbers to the nearest convenient figure and look at the suggested answers for the nearest to your estimate.

This section is divided into three parts: the first deals with the four rules, percentages and fractions; the second offers exercises in approximating; and the third consists of practical numerical problems.

1.   The four rules, percentages and fractions

Addition
See if you can work these out within **five** minutes.

1.	2 + 1 =	16.	0.5 + 3.6 =
2.	3 + 6 =	17.	10 + 10 + 20 =
3.	4 + 3 =	18.	100 + 5 + 200 =
4.	1 + 9 =	19.	1200 + 400 + 40 =
5.	10 + 1 =	20.	67 + 50 + 19 =
6.	11 + 7 =	21.	750 + 250 + 10 =
7.	16 + 8 =	22.	0.5 + 3.6 + 0.5 =
8.	11 + 16 =	23.	0.4 + 0.5 + 0.1 =
9.	69 + 0 =	24.	375 + 50 + 55 =
10.	36 + 10 =	25.	0.75 + 35 + 1.25 =
11.	0 + 0 =	26.	120 + 60 + 13 =
12.	120 + 30 =	27.	15 + 35 + 150 =
13.	1.1 + 1 =	28.	0.65 + 1.35 + 5 =
14.	1.5 + 1.5 =	29.	0.25 + 0.45 + 0.3 =
15.	10.5 + 10 =	30.	1.4 + 2.4 + 2.4 =

Subtraction
Now work these out.

1.	8 − 3 =	2.	12 − 9 =	3.	16 − 0 =
4.	71 − 29 =	5.	15.5 − 13.5 =	6.	10.66 − 8.3 =

7.	9654 – 3247	8.	8435 – 3253	9.	76540 – 47450

10.	63904 – 42615	11.	398004 – 75205	12.	6700.19 – 986.11

13.	506.65 – 45.37	14.	3020.26 – 543.88	15.	7021.03 – 1264.43

Now try to work these out in **three** minutes.

16.	70053 30536	17. 50605.03 4317.06	18.	900.802 625.837

If you cannot get these right in the suggested time you need further practice.

Multiplication
Work these out.

Simple multiplication

1.	5863 × 5	2.	950 × 4	3.	1637 × 3

4.	2486 × 4	5.	369 × 7

Long multiplication

6. 5689
    × 15
    ____
    ____

7. 5868
    × 17
    ____
    ____

8. 66085
    × 10
    ____
    ____

9. 2560919
    ×   205
    _____
    _____

10. 150897
    ×   350
    _____
    _____

Long multiplication with decimals

11. 60593
    × 3.2
    ____
    ____

12. 963.40
    ×   24
    ____
    ____

13. 76003
    × 96.05
    _____
    _____

Here is a useful tip: keep your calculation neat and the numbers aligned, otherwise you may add up the wrong columns.

Division
Work these out. Place your answers along the top of each sum.

Simple division

1.

4 ⟌ 12

2.

12 ⟌ 72

3.

8 ⟌ 56

4.

6 ⟌ 24

5.

5 ⟌ 950

6.

7 ⟌ 315

Long division (get help if you can't do these)

7.

$$17\overline{)1105}$$

8.

$$11\overline{)11220}$$

9.

$$16\overline{)7632}$$

Division with decimals

10.

$$25\overline{)330}$$

11.

$$12.2\overline{)140.3}$$

12.

$$17\overline{)209.1}$$

You have to practise a lot and know your tables before you become both quick and accurate at these exercises.

Division to time. You have **three** minutes.

1.

$$27\overline{)6048}$$

2.

$$12\overline{)126}$$

3.

$$18.4\overline{)465.52}$$

Percentages

Work these out.

1. 25% of 100 =
2. 30% of 70 =
3. 20% of 50 =
4. 90% of 25 =
5. 75% of 1000 =
6. 65% of 2560 =
7. ?% of 5500 = 3025
8. ?% of 7350 = 3454.50
9. 36% of ? = 243
10. 17% of ? = 14.79
11. ?% of 950 = 47.5
12. 3% of ? = 25.95
13. 6% of 66 =
14. If 6.8 is 8% what is 100%?
15. If 1.6 is 4% what is 100%?

Fractions

If you are applying for a technical job in telecommunications or engineering you may be asked to do fractions.

Work out the missing fraction or number.

1. $\frac{2}{2} = ?$

2. $\frac{4}{1} = ?$

3. $\frac{2}{4} = ?$

4. $\frac{30}{3} = ?$

5. $\frac{50}{?} = 10$

6. $\frac{?}{4} = 2$

Work these out.

7. $\frac{1}{2}$ of 28 =

8. $\frac{3}{4}$ of 20 = 5

9. $\frac{1}{3}$ of 60 = 2

10. $\frac{1}{4}$ of 100 =

If you cannot do these, ask for help.

Work these out.

11. $\frac{1}{4} + \frac{1}{3} + \frac{2}{6} =$

12. $1\frac{1}{2} + \frac{1}{6} + \frac{2}{3} =$

13. $6 \times \frac{3}{4} =$

14. $6\frac{1}{2} \times 5\frac{1}{4} =$

This is how hard these types of calculation are in real tests.

Try to do the next three examples in **three** minutes.

15. $1\frac{1}{2} + \frac{5}{6} + \frac{9}{12} =$ 16. $\frac{5}{6}$ of 192 =

17. $\frac{45}{9} \times 5 =$

If you got all three right in the three minutes, you ought to do well in a numerical test containing this sort of question.

Don't give up if you cannot do these. If you have time get help or enrol on a numeracy course at your local college of further education or adult education institute.

2.   Approximating

Rounding off numbers (1)

The purpose of this exercise is to help you make rough calculations quickly. This is particularly useful when you are presented with several answers and you have to choose one of them. By rounding off numbers and then doing the calculations you will have an answer that will be near enough to the correct answer.

First, we will ask you to round off to the nearest whole number. Later you will have the opportunity to do some calculations.

Now try the following.

Example: 2.89 is nearest to 3

1. 99.99   is nearest to. . . . .
2. 9.9   is nearest to. . . . .
3. 1.89   is nearest to. . . . .
4. 9.19   is nearest to. . . . .
5. 7.8   is nearest to. . . . .
6. 499.67   is nearest to. . . . .
7. 115.10   is nearest to. . . . .
8. 5.8892   is nearest to. . . . .
9. 3.12   is nearest to. . . . .

10. 6.2113   is nearest to......
11. 2.102   is nearest to......
12. 8.421   is nearest to......
13. 5.6110   is nearest to......
14. 7.9876   is nearest to......
15. 44.898   is nearest to......

Rounding off numbers (2)

In this exercise you have to convert the figures to the nearest convenient sum.

Example:
95% of 487 would become 100% of 500
29% of 291 would become 30% of 300

1. 19% of 694.............   9. 52% of 805..........
2. 87% of 55..............   10. 43% of 82...........
3. 52% of 59..............   11. 8.9% of 39.8.........
4. 20% of 987.............   12. 4.99% of 47.989......
5. 47% of 188.............   13. 4.965% of 98.932.....
6. 18% of 94..............   14. 119.5% of 999.659....
7. 192% of 106............   15. 9.98% of 699........
8. 9% of 888..............

Rounding off numbers (3)

In this exercise you should first round off the numbers before making the calculations, giving your answers in nearest whole numbers.

Example:

Add	6.983	is nearest to	7
	3.896	is nearest to	4
	1.883	is nearest to	2
Answer			13

Now try the following. Remember we only need the nearest answer, not the exact one.

1.	Add	5.8892 3.12 6.2113	2.	Add	449.67 99.99 1.89
3.	Subtract	9.9 1.89	4.	Subtract	499.67 199.76
5.	Multiply	99.68 1.95	6.	Multiply	6969.763 1.996

7. Divide 6969.763 by 1.996   _____

8. Divide 7998.687 by 3.893   _____

9. What is 10% of 9.99?   _____

10. What is 20% of 9.99?   _____

11. 3.321 + 4.1 + 10.1   _____

12. 699.76 + 99.89   _____

13. 699.76 – 99.89   _____

14. 9.9% of 49.789   _____

15. 49.9% of 9.9   _____

Addition

In this exercise you should approximate the answers as quickly as you can and then choose an answer from the box.

1. 0.49 + 399 + 49 =
2. 3098 + 2056 + 1078 =
3. 749 + 249 =
4. 2258.3 + 4934.1 + 5.2 =
5. 14.78 + 20.096 + 16.04 + 50 =
6. 1.5 + 59 + 39 + 50.5 =
7. 0.5 + 4.5 + 0.5 + 500.5 =
8. 509 + 309 + 209 + 203 =
9. 5035 + 6035 + 4030 =
10. 1559 + 2539 + 3332 =

7430	1230	15100
7709	448.49	6232
150	506	998
7197.6	100.916	200.919

Subtraction

Estimate the following:

You will be able to identify the correct answers far more quickly if you estimate rather than work out the calculations fully, round up figures to convenient sums, and look for the exact answers among those suggested in the box.

1. 139 – 17 =   2. 759 – 732 =   3. 9.87 – 7.95 =
4. 2987 – 499 =   5. 13.07 – 2.85 = 6. 634 – 171 =
7. 6278 – 1483 = 8. 555 – 326 =   9. 9987 – 399.12 =
10. 99.45 – 25.60 =

10.22	73.85	122
4795	27	1.92
463	9587.88	229
2488		

Multiplication

In this exercise you should approximate the answers as quickly as you can and then choose an answer from the box.

1. $59 \times 5 \times 5 =$
2. $78 \times 10 \times 19 =$
3. $2.5 \times 10 \times 5 =$
4. $55 \times 3 \times 10 =$
5. $500 \times 0.5 \times 10 =$
6. $55 \times 6 \times 0.5 =$
7. $100 \times 100 \times 1 =$
8. $200 \times 100 \times 1.5 =$
9. $100 \times 0.9999 =$
10. $100 \times 0.5 \times 0.999 =$

49.95	99.99	225
30000	335	10000
445	165	2500
1650	555	125
14820	1475	665

Division

Estimate the following and choose an answer from the box:

1.

$3 \overline{\smash{)}24.6}$

2.

$9 \overline{\smash{)}198}$

3

$596 \overline{\smash{)}1072.8}$

4.

$4.5 \overline{\smash{)}495}$

5.

$9.9 \overline{\smash{)}9801}$

100	990	8.2	22	1.8

Percentages

In this exercise you should approximate the answers as quickly as you can and then choose an answer from the box.

1. 10% of 500 =
2. 20% of 600 =
3. 33% of 999 =
4. 49% of 749 =
5. 5% of 5000 =
6. 29% of 695 =
7. 18% of 95.99 =
8. 16% of 450 =
9. 11% of 19000 =
10. 9% of 5000 =

250	450	645
2090	750	201.84
855	17.28	72
50	367.01	960
329.67	540	120

Fractions

Estimate the following and choose an answer from the box:

1. $\frac{1}{4}$ of 55 =

2. $\frac{1}{3}$ of 24 =

3. $\frac{2}{3}$ of 90 =

4. $\frac{1}{4}$ of 124 =

5. $\frac{1}{2} + \frac{1}{3} + 1\frac{1}{4} =$

8	60	$2^{1}/_{12}$	$13^{3}/_{4}$	31

Mixed

In this exercise you should approximate the answers. You should do this by rounding off the numbers and then roughly calculating the answer. Once you have done this, pick the correct answer from the box.

Now do these 12 questions in **five** minutes.

1.   29 + 41 + 29   2.   99 – 19

3.   19% of 49   4.   9 × 18

5.   395 ÷ 9   6.   0.9 + 89.1 – 14.6

7.   37% of 385   8.   845 ÷ 12

9.   456   10.   5678
          654   – 4567
         +123

11.   456   12.   20 = X% of 400
      ×12   What is X?

55	20	195
68	111	1111
1233	70.41	142.45
75.4	43.88	162
9.31	80	99
5472	4527	5

More percentages and some essential ratios

Try these further examples. Being confident, fast and accurate in these essential operations is key to success in psychometric tests today. So keep practising without a calculator. Explanations and answers are provided on page 223. If the percentage is reoccurring then work it to only one decimal place.

Changing fractions to percentages

Tip: To change a fraction to a percentage divide 100 by the bottom value and then multiply the outcome by the top value.

Q1   Find ½ as a percentage.   Answer

Q2   Find ¼ as a percentage.   Answer

Q3   Find $^1/_3$ as a percentage.   Answer

Q4   Find $^1/_5$ as a percentage.   Answer

Q5   Find $^1/_8$ as a percentage.   Answer

Q6   Find $^1/_{16}$ as a percentage.   Answer

Q7   Find $^1/_{12}$ as a percentage.   Answer

Q8   Find $^1/_9$ as a percentage.   Answer

Q9   Find $^2/_3$ as a percentage.   Answer

Q10   Find $^3/_5$ as a percentage.   Answer

Q11   Find $^6/_{16}$ as a percentage.   Answer

Q12   Find $^5/_8$ as a percentage.   Answer

Changing between decimals and percentages

Tip: Simply multiply a decimal by 100 to get the equivalent percentage and divide the percentage by 100 to get the equivalent decimal.

Q1   Convert 0.5 to a percentage.   Answer

Q2   Convert 0.2 to a percentage   Answer

Q3 Convert 0.6 to a percentage.

Answer

Q4 Convert 0.4 to a percentage.

Answer

Q5 Convert 0.35 to a percentage.

Answer

Q6 Convert 0.72 to a percentage.

Answer

Q7 Convert 0.425 to a percentage.

Answer

Q8 Convert 0.333 to a percentage.

Answer

Q9 Convert 0.5325 to a percentage.

Answer

Q10 Convert 25% to a decimal.

Answer

Q11 Convert 90% to a decimal.

Answer

Q12   Convert 5% to a decimal.   Answer

Q13   Convert 15% to a decimal.   Answer

Q14   Convert 2.4% to a decimal.   Answer

Q15   Convert 0.6% to a decimal.   Answer

A value expressed as a percentage of another

Tip: Write the first value as a percentage of the second and then convert the fraction into a percentage.

Q1   Find 15 as a percentage of 50.   Answer

Q2   Find 3 as a percentage of 25.   Answer

Q3   Find 5 as a percentage of 40.   Answer

Q4   Find 1 as a percentage of 5.

Answer

Q5   Find 6 as a percentage of 75.

Answer

Q6   Find 10 as a percentage of 12.5.

Answer

Q7   Find 2 as a percentage of 16.

Answer

Q8   Find 4 as a percentage of 80.

Answer

Q9   Find 12 as a percentage of 40.

Answer

Q10   Find 28 as a percentage of 70.

Answer

Finding percentages of quantities

Tip: Convert the percentage to a decimal and then multiply it by the quantity but be careful of the units.

Q1   Find 40% of £80.

Answer

Q2   Find 25% of 3 hours.

Answer

Q3   Find 15% of 40 metres.

Answer

Q4   Find 20% of £9.

Answer

Q5   Find 5% of 12 metres.

Answer

Q6   Find 10% of 12 hours.

Answer

Q7   Find 15% of £520.

Answer

Q8   Find 30% of 1 hour 30 minutes.

Answer

Q9   Find 20% of 18.3 metres.

Answer

Q10   Find 17.5% of 5 hours.   Answer

Percentage increase

Tip: Percentage increase is calculated by dividing the increase by the original amount and multiplying the answer by 100.

Q1   What is the percentage increase between 20 and 30?

Answer

Q2   What is the percentage increase between 40 and 48?

Answer

Q3   What is the percentage increase between 18 and 24?

Answer

Q4   What is the percentage increase between 80 and 112?

Answer

Q5   What is the percentage increase between 11 and 17.6?

Answer

Q6   What is the percentage increase between 25 and 32.5?

Answer

Q7   What is the percentage increase between 90 and 97.2?

Answer

Q8   What is the percentage increase between 8 and 9?

Answer

Q9   What is the percentage increase between 120 and 124.8?

Answer

Q10   What is the percentage increase between 36 and 57.6?

Answer

Percentage decrease

Tip: Work out percentage decrease by dividing the amount of decrease by the original amount and multiplying the answer by 100.

Q1   What is the percentage decrease between 100 and 95?

Answer

Q2   What is the percentage decrease between 50 and 42?

Answer

Q3   What is the percentage decrease between 75 and 57?

Answer

Q4   What is the percentage decrease between 80 and 44?

Answer

Q5   What is the percentage decrease between 120 and 48?

Answer

Q6   What is the percentage decrease between 8 and 2?

Answer

Q7   What is the percentage decrease between 90 and 9?

Answer

Q8   What is the percentage decrease between 25 and 17.5?

Answer

Q9   What is the percentage decrease between 30 and 26.4?

Answer

Q10   What is the percentage decrease between 65 and 50.7?

Answer

Percentage profit or loss

Tip: To calculate the percentage profit divide the amount of profit by the buying price and multiply the answer by 100; to calculate the percentage loss divide the loss by the buying price and multiply the answer by 100. Don't forget to state whether the answer is a profit or loss.

Q1   What is the percentage profit or loss if the buying price of an item was £10 and the selling price was £12?

Answer

Q2   What is the percentage profit or loss if the buying price of an item was £40 and the selling price was £32?

Answer

Q3   What is the percentage profit or loss if the buying price of an item was £50 and the selling price was £70?

Answer

Q4   What is the percentage profit or loss if the buying price of an
item was £8 and the selling price was £7?

Answer

Q5   What is the percentage profit or loss if the buying price of an
item was £25 and the selling price was £32.50?

Answer

Q6   What is the percentage profit or loss if the buying price of an
item was £12 and the selling price was £2.40?

Answer

Q7   What is the percentage profit or loss if the buying price of an
item was £5 and the selling price was £5.75?

Answer

Q8   What is the percentage profit or loss if the buying price of an
item was £45 and the selling price was £13.5?

Answer

Q9   What is the percentage profit or loss if the buying price of an
item was £70 and the selling price was £112?

Answer

Q10   What is the percentage profit or loss if the buying price of an item was £6.50 and the selling price was £6.11?

Answer

Ratios

Tip: To divide a sum by a ratio add together all the parts of the ratio, divide the amount by the answer; this gives you the value of each part, then calculate each share by multiplying the value of each part by the number of parts.

Q1   Divide 100 into the ratio 4 : 1.

Answer

Q2   Divide 49 into the ratio 3 : 4.

Answer

Q3   Divide 36 into the ratio 1 : 5.

Answer

Q4   Divide 72 into the ratio 5 : 3.

Answer

Q5   Divide 55 into the ratio 3 : 2.   Answer

Q6   Divide 130 into the ratio 1 : 7 : 2.   Answer

Q7   Divide 52 into the ratio 6 : 4 : 3.   Answer

Q8   Divide 55 into the ratio 7 : 3 : 12.   Answer

Q9   Divide 28 into the ratio 1 : 4 : 3.   Answer

Q10   Divide 60.5 into the ratio 3 : 5 : 4.   Answer

3.   Practical numerical problems

Work these out without the use of a calculator.

1. Twenty-seven people are asked to contribute 50 pence each towards the cost of a leaving present for a colleague but three decline; how much is collected?

Answer

2. Your telephone bill comprises a standing charge of £7.93, £40.47 worth of calls and £7.26 of value added tax. What is the total?

Answer

3. Nicky works flexi-time and is contracted to work a 35-hour week. For three weeks she has only worked 27½ hours a week. How many hours does she owe?

Answer

Work towards getting this sort of sum right consistently and quickly.

4. A large company employs 15% of the working population in a small town. The total population of the town is 70,000, of which 50% is the working population. How many people are employed by the company?

Answer

5. A shop sells washing machines for £150 plus VAT at 17.5%. What is the total price that customers would have to pay?

Answer

6. The same shop has a special offer on a video and television when bought together. The combined price is £650 inclusive, less a discount of 12%. What is the special offer price?

Answer

7. A clerical officer earns £12,000 gross per year. She is entitled to a tax-free personal allowance of £3000 and pays income tax at 25% on the balance. What is her net pay per year?

Answer

8. A senior clerical officer earns £15,000. What is the annual net pay, assuming all the other information is as above?

Answer

9. A businessperson buys 500 pairs of shoes at a cost of £5000. He wants to make a 30% profit. What is the price he should charge for a pair of shoes?

Answer

10. A woman buys a television for £550, a CD player for £450, a computer for £850. She gets a 10% discount from the total price. How much has she paid?

Answer

If her two sons contribute two-thirds of the total cost, what would be the woman's share of the cost?

Answer

11. If Michael has £50, Chris has 50% more than Michael, and Betty has only half as much as Chris, how much money does Betty have?

Answer

12. An employer has 60 people working for her and she wants to give a 15% bonus to all her staff. How much would each staff member receive if the total weekly wage bill is normally £15,000?

Answer

13. How much would each staff member receive if the bonus is reduced to 10%?

Answer

14. Claire earns £430.60 per week but £86.12 income tax and £43.60 National Insurance contributions are deducted. How much net pay does she receive?

Answer

Timed practical numerical problems
Over the page you will find three more of these exercises to be done
against time. You have **three** minutes.

Do not turn the page to begin the timed exercise until you are ready.

1. A restaurant bill totals £42.80 and is to be divided between four
    people. How much has each person to pay?

    Answer

2. How much value added tax, charged at 17.5%, would be added
    to a pre-tax total of £88?

    Answer

3. If a 2 kilowatt electric fire costs 10.7 pence an hour to run, how
    much would it cost to operate a 1 kilowatt fire for 16 hours?

    Answer

Your speed and accuracy at this sort of calculation will greatly
improve with practice.

Foreign currency exchange rates

Here is a table of different foreign currencies. The values shown are equal to £1 sterling. For example: £1 = 10 francs. (We are aware that many of these currencies no longer exist.)

French francs	10
Dutch guilders	5
Italian lire	2500
German marks	3
US dollars	1.80
Indian rupees	65

Using the above exchange rates to calculate the following:

1. A customer wishes to purchase 390 German marks. How many pounds will she have to pay?

    A. 390   B. 230   C. 190   D. 130   E. None of these

2. How many Indian rupees can you get for £350?

    A. 600   B. 6500   C. 7500   D. 5650   E. None of these

3. How many pounds would you get for 126 francs?

    A. 10   B. 15   C. 12.60   D. 10.50   E. None of these

4. What are 500 guilders worth in German marks?

    A. 100   B. 200   C. 300   D. 400   E. None of these

5. Convert 250,000 lire into Indian rupees. How many rupees is that?

    A. 1250   B. 6500   C. 2500   D. 100   E. None of these

6. If you bought 90 US dollars and 600 French francs, how many pounds would you require?

    A. 250   B. 150   C. 125   D. 110   E. None of these

French francs	10
Dutch guilders	5
Italian lire	2500
German marks	3
US dollars	1.80
Indian rupees	65

7. A tourist has £500 with which he intends to purchase some foreign currencies. He decides to buy francs for 25% of the pounds, marks for a further 25% and with the remaining 50% of the pounds he decides to buy Italian lire. What are the different amounts of currencies that the tourist will get?

	A.	B.	C.	D.	E.
francs	1600	1300	1400	1250	None
marks	375	475	275	375	of
lire	625,000	635,000	625,000	625,000	these

8. A woman returning from a holiday finds that she still has some foreign money left. She has 300 Dutch guilders, 500 US dollars and 50 francs in change, which she is not able to exchange. What is the total amount of pounds she will get?

A. 377.78 B. 337.78 C. 327.78 D. 347.78 E. None of these

9. A French tourist wishes to buy 850 dollars. How many francs will that cost him?

A. 7566.67 B. 5056.67 C. 4722.22 D. 6666.67
E. None of these

10. An American brings 7200 dollars with her to London and wants to exchange them for pounds. How many pounds would she get after paying a 10% commission charge?

A. 2600   B. 3600   C. 4600   D. 5600   E. None of these

Clerical tests

These exercises will help in your preparation for the types of selection test that companies use to assess your suitability for clerical work and work with computers.

1.   Coded instructions

These involve sets of rules or tables of information that you interpret and then apply to a series of situations or refer to in order to answer a series of questions.

Exercise 1
Establish from the table the answers to the questions.

Time	What happened	Where we were
9 am	the telephone rang	out shopping
12.00	the post arrived	watching the news on TV
1 pm	I paid the milk bill	on the door step
2 pm	did the washing	down the launderette
4 pm	cooked dinner	in the kitchen

Questions

1.   Where was I at 2 pm? _____

2.   What was I doing at 12.00?_____

3.   What time was it when I was watching TV? _____

4.   What was I doing while on the door step?_____

5.   When did the post arrive? _____

6.   What time did the phone ring? _____

Exercise 2

In this exercise you are required to translate the English sentences into the code equivalents by referring to the dictionary.

Dictionary

call	=	ranch
Fido	=	Tratma
dog	=	lippgai
is	=	nitco
black	=	modod
the	=	udyne

Example:

Call Fido = Ranch Tratma

Questions

1. The dog is black. _____
2. Fido is the dog. _____
3. Call the black dog. _____

Now translate these coded sentences into English.

1. Tratma udyne lippgai. _____
2. Nitco Tratma modod? _____
3. Nitco udyne lippgai Tratma? _____

Exercise 3
Computerised accounts system for a building society

Codes

Current account	C
Share account	S
Fixed account	F
Loan account	L

The code for the type of account is followed by an account number and a code indicating whether the account is in credit or overdrawn.

Account in credit	OC
Account overdrawn	OD

Example:

A fixed account number 00210 in credit = F00210OC

Answer the following questions by selecting one of the suggested answers A, B, C or D. Indicate your answer by writing either A, B, C or D in the answer box.

Questions

1.   A current account number 3679830 in credit.

A.   S367830OC
B.   L3679830OC
C.   C33679830OC
D.   C3679830OC

Answer

2. A share account number 2213730 overdrawn.

A. L2213730OC
B. S2213730OD
C. F2213730OC
D. C2213730OD

Answer

3. A loan account number 087231 in credit.
A. C087231OD
B. S087231OC
C. L087231OD
D. L087231OC

Answer

Timed coded instructions exercise
Over the page is a timed coded instructions exercise. Allow yourself
five minutes to answer the five questions.

Do not turn the page until you are ready to do the timed exercise.

A computerised till in a shop

If payment is made by credit card it is coded CT.

Payment by cheque is coded CHQ.

For cash the code is CS.

If the amount is less than £50 the letter U follows the code.

If the amount is over £50 the letter O follows the code.

For all furniture items the number 1 follows the letter U or O.

Other goods are numbered 2.

Answer the following questions by selecting one of the suggested answers. Indicate your answer by writing A, B, C or D in the answer box.

Example:

A man buys a suit for £150 and pays by credit card.

A. CTO1
B. CTU1
C. CTO2
D. CTU2

Answer

C

1. A couple buy a dining table for £99 and pay cash.

A. CS
B. CHQ
C. CS2
D. CSO1

Answer

2. A woman buys a shirt for £25 and pays by cheque.

A. CHQ
B. CGQ1
C. CHQ2
D. CHQU2

Answer

3. A man buys a chair for £49.99 and pays by credit card.

A. CTO1
B. CTU1
C. CTO2
D. CSU2

Answer

4. A bed is bought for £250 cash.

A. CTQ1
B. CTU1
C. CTO2
D. CSO1

Answer

5. Someone writes a cheque out to the value of £199.95 in payment of a colour TV.

A. CTU2
B. CSO1
C. CQHU2
D. CHQO2

Answer

END OF EXERCISE

More examples of this type of question can be found in the Kogan Page title, *How to Pass Computer Selection Tests*.

Exercise 4

1. There are six friends and their ages are as follows – two are 14 years of age, another two are 15 and the last two are 16.

    What is their average age?

    Answer

2. A person going to work walks for five minutes, waits for a bus for three minutes and is on the bus for 10 minutes. A walk from the bus stop to the train station takes seven minutes. The train journey is 30 minutes and the walk to the office from the train station is another eight minutes.

    How long does it take for the whole journey?

    Answer

3. A man buys the following items from a green grocer, 1 kilo of apples, 500 grams of bananas, 350 grams of oranges, 1½ kilos of potatoes and 250 grams of tomatoes.

    What is the total weight of all these items?

    Answer

4. Neha is six years younger than Raheel. Raheel is two years older than Adeel and Uzair. Simrun is four years old. The difference in age between Simrun and Adeel is seven years.

    How old is Neha?

    Answer

5. A box can hold 720 packets of sugar and there are 24 such boxes. What is the total number of packets?

Answer

6. A person buys seven items from a supermarket and the cost of these items is £10.50. What is the average price of each item?

Answer

7. An electrician has 8m of cable. If she uses 2.36m, how much will she have left?

Answer

8. Neha and Simrun have a combined weight of 141.50kg. If Simrun weighs 68.40kg, what is Neha's weight?

Answer

9. Raheel and Adeel have a combined height of 3.74m. Raheel is 24cm taller than Adeel. What are their respective heights?

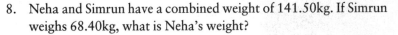

Raheel   Answer

Adeel   Answer

10. Adam earns £15,450, John earns £ 14,250, Jamie earns £18,325 and Tom earns £19,175. Calculate the total and the average salary.

Answer

11. A computer operator is able to input 120 characters per minute using a standard keyboard. How many characters can be typed in half an hour?

Answer

12. A company employs 500 people, of whom 20% are men. How many women work there?

Answer

13. If a computer model A costs £600, model B costs 50% more than model A and model C costs half the price of model B, how much does model C cost?

Answer

14. A businessperson buys 20 computers at a cost of £10,000. He wants to make a 20% profit on the computers. How much should he sell each computer at?

Answer

15. John gives three-quarters of his sweets to Julie, and Julie gives a third of this amount to Mike. If Mike receives nine sweets, how many sweets did John start with?

Answer

Exercise 5

In this exercise you are required to carry out calculations. However, instead of numbers you are presented with letters. Each letter is given a value, but your answer will be in number format.

Let: $A = 2$ $B = 3$ $C = 4$ $D = 5$

Example question:

$A + B = ?$

In this case the answer is 5 because $A = 2$ and $B = 3$, therefore $2 + 3 = 5$.

Remember that all calculations within brackets have to be carried out first.

Now work out the following:

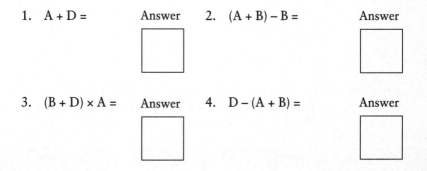

1. $A + D =$ Answer   2. $(A + B) - B =$ Answer

3. $(B + D) \times A =$ Answer   4. $D - (A + B) =$ Answer

5. $(D \times B) - D =$ Answer   6. $A + B + C - D =$ Answer

7. $(D + C + B) \div A =$ Answer   8. $(C \times D) + (A \times B) =$ Answer

9. $(B \times C) - (A + C) =$ Answer   10. $B + C + D - A =$ Answer

Exercise 6
Let: $A = 5$ $B = 8$ $C = 14$ $D = 16$

1. $(B + C) \times A =$ Answer   2. $(C - B) \times D =$ Answer

3. $(D - A) - (C - B) =$ Answer   4. $(D - C) \times (A + B) =$ Answer

Exercise 7
In this exercise you will be presented with numerical problems that are represented by letters. Each letter has been given a value that corresponds with its position in the alphabet. Thus 'A' =1 and 'Z' = 26.

Give your answers as letters.

Example question:

A + B = ?

A = 1 B = 2 C = 3 D = 4 etc. Therefore A(1) + B(2) = C(3)

Hint: You will find it helpful to write down the alphabet somewhere and to number each letter.

1. F + ? = P   Answer

2. C + ? = J   Answer

3. L + D = ?   Answer

4. Z – B = ?   Answer

5. ? × K = V   Answer

6. C + D + ? = N   Answer

7. R – H = ?   Answer

8. $P + A - G = ?$ Answer

9. $V + W - Z = ?$ Answer

10. $T \times E / D = ?$ Answer

11. $J \times B / ? = A$ Answer

12. $F \times ? - J = Z$ Answer

13. $Y + ? - T = Z$ Answer

14. $R + P - L = ?$ Answer

15. $(C + D) \times ? = U$ Answer

For this part of the exercise please give the answers in numbers.

16. $(P + N) \times E = ?$ Answer

17. $(Z / B) \times L = ?$ Answer

18. $V + H + R - T ?$ Answer

19. $(E \times Y+Y) / B = ?$ Answer

20. $T + (U / C) = ?$ Answer

Exercise 8
Constructing equations

In this exercise your task is to arrange the numbers and arithmetic symbols, presented below, to make true equations. You are then to choose a number from the list on the right that gives you a correct answer.

Symbols used are: Plus (+), Minus (−), Multiply (×) and Divide (/)

Example questions:

1. 1 2 3 + −   A) 0   B) 3   C) 5   D) 6   E) 1

2. 2 3 4 + ×   A) 20   B) 16   C) 12   D) 10   E) 8

The answers to the example questions are:

1. $1 + 2 - 3 = 0$ The answer is A.

We could have written the equation thus:

$3 + 2 - 1 = 4$

However, this is not available in the answer list.

2. $2 \times 3 + 4 = 10$ The answer is D.

NOW TRY THE FOLLOWING QUESTIONS

1. 5 3 1	+ −	A) 6	B) 5	C) 4	D) 3	E) 2
2. 9 6 7	+ −	A) 10	B) 11	C) 12	D) 6	E) 7
3. 8 4 5	+ −	A) 4	B) 5	C) 6	D) 7	E) 8
4. 2 3 4 5	+ + −	A) 3	B) 4	C) 5	D) 7	E) 9
5. 6 1 8 9	+ + −	A) 9	B) 10	C) 12	D) 14	E) 6
6. 2 4 6	× −	A) 0	B) 18	C) 20	D) 10	E) 2
7. 7 3 1	× −	A) 1	B) 3	C) 4	D) 7	E) 21
8. 9 1 2	+ +	A) 9	B) 10	C) 11	D) 12	E) 13
9. 1 1 2	+ −	A) 1	B) 5	C) 3	D) 2	E) 4
10. 3 5 7 9	× + −	A) 17	B) 18	C) 28	D) 24	E) 60

Exercise 9

In this exercise you have to write the missing sign in the box so that the vertical and horizontal answers are equal. Look at the example below.

Example:

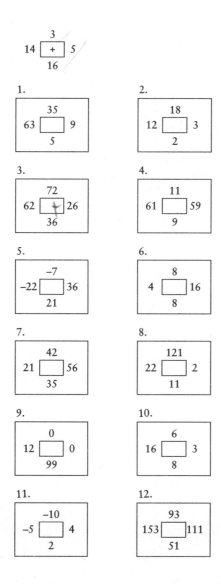

```
      3
14 [ + ] 5
     16
```

1.
```
     35
63 [   ] 9
      5
```

2.
```
      18
12 [   ] 3
       2
```

3.
```
     72
62 [   ] 26
     36
```

4.
```
     11
61 [   ] 59
      9
```

5.
```
     −7
−22 [   ] 36
      21
```

6.
```
      8
4 [   ] 16
      8
```

7.
```
     42
21 [   ] 56
     35
```

8.
```
     121
22 [   ] 2
      11
```

9.
```
      0
12 [   ] 0
      99
```

10.
```
      6
16 [   ] 3
      8
```

11.
```
     −10
−5 [   ] 4
      2
```

12.
```
      93
153 [   ] 111
      51
```

Exercise 10

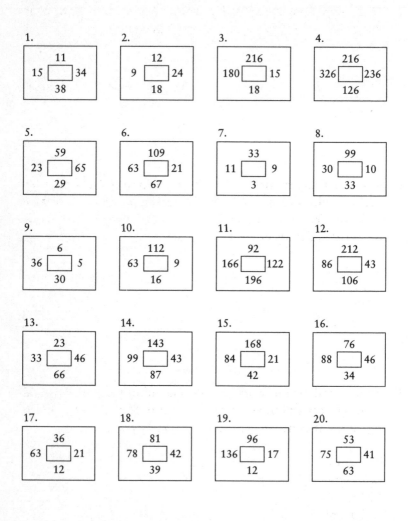

1.
```
      11
 15 [   ] 34
      38
```

2.
```
      12
  9 [   ] 24
      18
```

3.
```
      216
 180 [   ] 15
      18
```

4.
```
      216
 326 [   ] 236
      126
```

5.
```
      59
 23 [   ] 65
      29
```

6.
```
      109
 63 [   ] 21
      67
```

7.
```
      33
 11 [   ] 9
      3
```

8.
```
      99
 30 [   ] 10
      33
```

9.
```
      6
 36 [   ] 5
      30
```

10.
```
      112
 63 [   ] 9
      16
```

11.
```
      92
 166 [   ] 122
      196
```

12.
```
      212
 86 [   ] 43
      106
```

13.
```
      23
 33 [   ] 46
      66
```

14.
```
      143
 99 [   ] 43
      87
```

15.
```
      168
 84 [   ] 21
      42
```

16.
```
      76
 88 [   ] 46
      34
```

17.
```
      36
 63 [   ] 21
      12
```

18.
```
      81
 78 [   ] 42
      39
```

19.
```
      96
 136 [   ] 17
      12
```

20.
```
      53
 75 [   ] 41
      63
```

Exercise 11

1. If you were using a map with a scale of 5cm to 1km, how many kilometres would be represented by 75cm on the map?

    A. 5km
    B. 10km
    C. 15km
    D. 75km

    Answer

2. Tim and Tom are friends. They plan a trip to the seaside. They decide to hire a car for the day. The seaside is 79km from where they live. The cost of hiring the car is £45 plus 15p per km. How much will it cost them for the round trip?

    A. £45.15
    B. £58.70
    C. £68.70
    D. £90.30

    Answer

3. They then decide to work out the amount of petrol they would need. The car will travel 15.5km on 1 litre of petrol. How much petrol will they need to the nearest whole litre?

    A. 5 litres
    B. 10 litres
    C. 15 litres
    D. 20 litres

    Answer

4. Tim and Tom decide to have a party. They invited 80 people. But 10% of them said they could not come. A quarter of all those who said they would come did not come. How many people came to the party?

    A. 24
    B. 38
    C. 46
    D. 54

Answer

5. Tim and Tom want to send a parcel of old clothes to a charity. They have four boxes to choose from. They want the box with the biggest volume. Which of these has the biggest volume?

    A. 70cm × 55cm × 35cm
    B. 70cm × 60cm × 30cm
    C. 80cm × 60cm × 20cm
    D. 80cm × 55cm × 20cm

Answer

A teacher asked the pupils in her tutor group to say how many hours they watched television per week. Once she had collected the data she then produced a chart to display the results. Use the chart to answer questions 6 to 9.

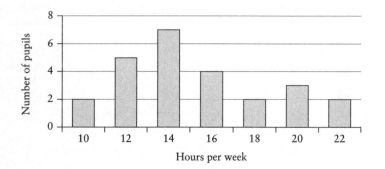

6. How many pupils are there in the class?

    A. 7
    B. 22
    C. 25
    D. None of the above

    Answer

7. What is the average time spent watching television (to the nearest hour)?

    A. 4 hours
    B. 6 hours
    C. 14 hours
    D. 16 hours

    Answer

8. How many pupils watch 20 or more hours of television per week?

    A. 2
    B. 3
    C. 4
    D. 5

    Answer

9. How many pupils watch television for under 16 hours per week?

    A. 10
    B. 12
    C. 14
    D. 16

    Answer

The table below shows all the animals on a farm

Use the information to answer questions 10 to 14.

Types of animal	Cows	Sheep	Pigs	Hens	Dogs	Horses
Number	30	90	60	25	3	2

10. How many cows, sheep and pigs does the farm have?

    A. 160
    B. 180
    C. 260
    D. 280

Answer

11. What fraction of the total number of animals on the farm are cows?

    A. $1/5$
    B. $1/6$
    C. $1/7$
    D. $1/8$

Answer

12. What is the ratio of cows to pigs?

    A. 1:2
    B. 1:3
    C. 1:4
    D. 1:5

Answer

13. What is the ratio of cows to sheep?

    A. 1 : 2
    B. 1 : 3
    C. 1 : 4
    D. 1 : 5

Answer

14. What is the ratio of horses to cows?

    A. 1:12
    B. 1:13
    C. 1:14
    D. 1:15

Answer

15. A new nursery is being opened. They plan to take in 40 children. The ratio of 1 : 4 is required. How many nursery teachers will they need?

    A. 5
    B. 10
    C. 15
    D. 20

Answer

A holiday guide has provided a table that shows the number of hours of sunshine on a Greek Island.

Use the table to answer questions 16 to 20 (you may need to find out the meaning of the following mathematical terms: mean, mode and median).

Month	Feb	Mar	April	May	June	July	Aug	Sept	Oct
Hours of sunshine – daily	6	7	8	9	11	12	10	9	9

16. What is the range of the daily hours of sunshine over the months shown?

    A. 5

    B. 6

    C. 7

    D. 8

Answer

17. What is the mean of the daily hours of sunshine for the months shown?

    A. 7

    B. 8

    C. 9

    D. 12

Answer

18. What is the median of the daily hours of sunshine for the months shown?

    A. 7

    B. 8

    C. 9

    D. 10

Answer

19. What is the mode of the daily hours of sunshine for the months shown?

A. 6
B. 7
C. 8
D. 9

Answer

20. Which of the following numbers is the biggest?

A. 1.067
B. 1.60
C. 1.67
D. 1.607

Answer

Exercise 12

In this exercise you are required to find the missing number from one of the boxes. The numbers are in some kind of a sequence, and it is your task to find that sequence in order to answer the question. The sequence may be horizontal or vertical.

1.

1	?	5
2	4	6

A)1 B)2 C)3 D)4 E)5

2.

2	?	8
16	32	64

A)6 B)4 C)3 D)5 E)10

3.

3	9	27
?	243	729

A)61 B)90 C)81 D)101 E)141

4.

6	12	?
48	96	192

A)18 B)20 C)22 D)24 E)36

5.

2	20	15
4	?	30

A)10 B)40 C)8 D)16 E)18

6.

5	15	30
?	75	105

A)45 B)70 C)50 D)65 E)60

7.

1	6	12
19	27	?

A)35 B)40 C)46 D)36 E)34

8.

1	6	15
3	9	?

A)19 B)20 C)21 D)27 E)30

9.

3	12	27
7	17	?

A)37 B)36 C)34 D)33 E)31

10.

?	15	45
1	3	9

A)3 B)4 C)5 D)6 E)7

Flow diagrams

These exercises require you to interpret the information presented and use it to answer the questions.

Exercise 1.   A catalogue order procedure

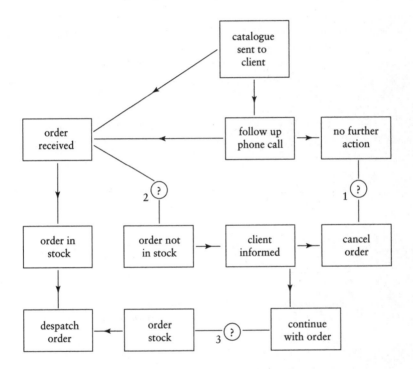

Study the flow diagram and decide which way the arrows ought to be drawn at points 1, 2 and 3. Indicate your answer by drawing arrows in the answer boxes provided.

1.

Answer

2.

Answer

3.

Answer

Exercise 2.   A finance department's invoice system

Interpret the flow diagram and answer the questions.

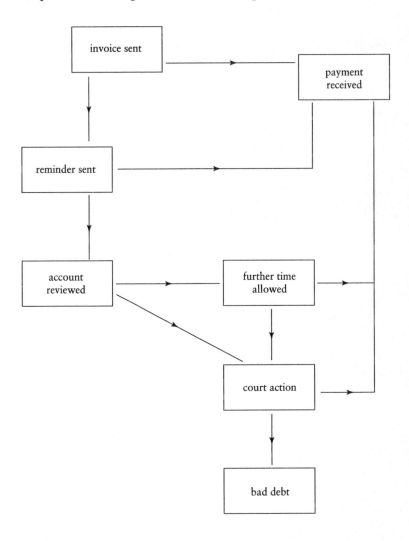

1. It was decided at the account review to give a customer extra time to pay but that time has now passed without result. What action should the accounts manager initiate?

Answer

_____

2. No payment has been received for an invoice. What action should be taken?

Answer

_____

3. If a reminder is sent after 30 days and the account review held after a further 30 days, what is the minimum period before court action is instigated?

Answer

_____

Timed flow diagram exercise

Over the page is a timed flow diagram exercise. Allow yourself **five** minutes to answer the five questions.

Do not turn the page until you are ready to do the timed exercise.

The recruitment process of a leading employer

You have **five** minutes in which to study the flow diagram and answer the questions.

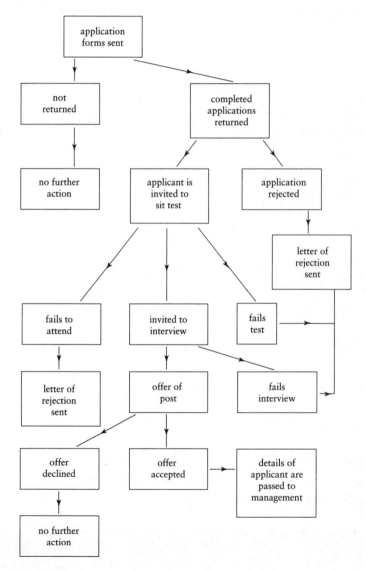

Indicate what the personnel officer should do if:

1. Someone fails to attend for interview.

Answer

_____

2. A candidate fails to return an application form.

Answer

_____

3. A candidate is successful at interview.

Answer

_____

4. A candidate submits a successful application form.

Answer

_____

5. A candidate accepts the offer of a post.

Answer

_____

END OF EXERCISE

3. Checking

In this exercise you are presented with a list of company names. On the left is the original list and on the right is a retyped version. Your task is to check the retyped version for any errors by comparing it with the original list on the left. Put brackets around the retyped version if there is an error.

Exercise 1
This exercise aims to assess your skills in checking speedily and accurately. Now complete this task in **three** minutes.

Original	Copy
Paine Chocolates	Pain Chocolates
Pall Mall Dispensing	Pall Mall Dispensing
Lodge Insurance Brokers	Lodge Insurence Brokers
Lodder Est Agts	LOdder Est Agts
Mill Hill Dry Clnrs	Mill Hill Dry Clnrs
Kahn Printers	Kahn Printers
Italian Piano Co	Italian Piano Co
Hoxtex Restaurants	Hoxtex Restaurant
Apollo Bed and Breakfast	Apollo Bedand Breakfast
Holloway Carpenters	Holloway Carpenters
Archway Halal Meat	Archway Hala Meat
Hookway Jewellers	Hookway Jewellers
Hi-tec School of Motoring	Hi-tec School of Motoring
Totland Hire Centre	Totland Hire Center
George's Recruitment	Georges Recruitment
West End Consultants	West End Consultants
Court Cars	Court cars
House of Lighting	Hourse of Lighting
Woxton Water Works	Woxton Water Works
Castletown Restaurants	Castletown Recruitments
Hardwood Doors Group Ltd	Hardwood Doors Group LTD
Mike's Do It Yourself Centre	Mike's Do It Yourself Centre
MITAKA Publishing House	MITAKA Publsihing House
Sunchung Takeaway	Sanchung Takeaway

Move Motorcycle Hire	Move Motorcyycle Hire
Portman Car and Van Rental	Portman Carr and Van Rental
Heitman and Son Accountants	Heitman and son Accountance
Ace Consulting Engineers	Ace Consulting Engineers ⌐
Hot Tandoori House	Hot Tundoori House
Safe Security Ltd	Safe security Ltd

Exercise 2

Original	*Copy*
ABC123	ABC123 ✓
ACCB/123/321	ACCB/123/321 ✓
CENTIMETRES/CUBIC	CENTEMETRES/CUBIC
GUMPTION	GUMPTION ✓
MEASURES/CAPACITY	MAESURES/CAPACITY
987654321/123456789	987654321/123456789 ✓
987/123/654/456:	987/123/654/456.
GERMANIUM-72.59	GERMÁNUM-72.59
MOLYBDENUM-95.94	MOLYBDENUM-95.94 ✓
NICKEL-58.71	NICKLE-58.71
ZIRCONIUM-91.22	ZIRCONIUM-91.22
PHOSPHORUS-30.9738	PHOSPHOROS-30.9738
MILLILITRES-36966	MILLILITERS-36966
MANGANESE-54.9380	MANGANESE-54.9380 ✓
DECAGRAMMES-15432	DECAGRAMMS-15432
KILOGRAMME-2205	KILOGRAMMES-2205
ANTIMONY-121.75	ANTIMONY-121.75
HYDROGEN-1.0080(H)	HYDROGIN-1.0080(H)
CHROMIUM-51.996	CHROMUIM-51.996
MINNESOTA STATE	MINNISOTA STATE
ZEDEKIAH	ZEDEKIAH ✓
WYOMING/CHEYENNE	WYCOMING/CHEYENNE
TENNESSEE/NASHVILLE	TENESSEE/NASHVILLE
ZOROASTER	ZOROASTER ✓
PENNSYLVANIA/H'BURG	PENNCYLVANIA/H'BURG

WHISTLER	WHISLER
VERSAILLES	VERSAILES
VERRUCOSE	VERRUCOSE ✓
UNHALLOWED	UNIHALLOWED
TREACHEROUS	TREACHEROUS ✓
TREASURY	TREASUERY
SPARE-PART	SPAIRE-PART
ROUSSEAU	RUOSSEAU ✓
EQUIVALENTS	EQIUVALENTS
FLOUNCE	FLUONCE ✓
HARDENBERG	HARDENBERG

Exercise 3

Original	*Copy*
123/456/789/AC	123/456/789/AC ✓
987/654/321/CA	987/654/321/CA ✓
32323/452/CIC	32332/452/CIC
ACEG/818/658	ACEG/818/658 ✓
BDFH/4653/12	BDFH)4653/12
ZED/678/TLT/010	ZED/678/TLT/010 ✓
WORLD/VIEW/83	WORLD/VEIW/83
ZEBEDEE/F/JJ	ZEBFDEE/F/JJ
YETI/SNOW/MAN	YETI/SNOW/MAN ✓
ORI/GIN/AL/212	ORI/GIN/AL/212 ✓
ADVERTISEMENT	ADVERITISEMENT
PERSONNEL/DEPT	PERSENNEL/DEPT
COM/PUT/ER/SYS/TEM	COM/PUT/ER/SyS/TEM
00/11/22/345/678	00/11/22/345/678
3456/0987/4321/32	3456/0987/4321/32 ✓
RO/AD/RU/NN/ER/234	RO/AD/RV/NN/ER/234
GAL/2001/200001/00	GAL/2001/20001/00
ISBN 0–561–15163–0	ISBN 0–561–15163–0 ✓
1010101/02020/300	1010101/02020/300 ✓
DATA-100/303/404/50	DATA/100/303/404/50

4.   Coded instructions (2)

To enter the computer, type	LOG/SYS
To use the word processing package, type	WP
To use the database package, type	DB
To use the spreadsheets package, type	SPS
To open a new file, type	OF/NAME
To open and edit an old file, type	EF/NAME
To delete a file, type	DF/NAME

Example:

To enter the computer and edit an old database file
Answer: LOG/SYS/DB/EF/NAME

Now try these (circle the correct answer):

Which code should be used for the following?

1.   To enter the computer

    [1]   SYS/LOG
    [2]   EF/NAME/LOG/SYS
    [3]   LOG/SYS
    [4]   ON/COM/PU/TER
    [5]   None of these

2.   To delete a file from the database (assume you have already entered the computer)

    [1]   DF/NAMEDB
    [2]   DB/DF/NAME
    [3]   DF/NAME/DB
    [4]   DF/NAME/SPS/WP/DB
    [5]   None of these

3.   To enter the computer and create a new file on the word processor

    [1]   OF/NAME/WP
    [2]   OF/NAME/LOG/WP
    [3]   LOG/WP/NAME/OF
    [4]   LOG/SYS/WP/OF/NAME
    [5]   None of these

4. To edit a spreadsheet file by entering the computer first

    [1]   ED/SPS/LOG/SYS
    [2]   EF/NAME/SPS/LOG/SYS
    [3]   LOG/SYS/EF/SPS/NAME
    [4]   LOG/SYS/SPS/OF/NAME
    [5]   None of these

5. To delete a file from the word processing package

    [1]   WP/EF/NAME/WP
    [2]   DF/NAME/WP
    [3]   WP/OF/NAME/
    [4]   DF/LOG/NAME
    [5]   None of these

6. To enter the computer and use the spreadsheets program

    [1]   LOG/SYS/USE
    [2]   LOG/SYS/SPS
    [3]   USE/SPS/COM/PUT/ER
    [4]   LOG/SPS/NAME
    [5]   None of these

7. To use the database by logging on to the system

    [1]   DB/LOG/SYS
    [2]   LOG/DB/ON/TO/SYS
    [3]   LOG/SYS/SPS
    [4]   LOG/SYS/DB
    [5]   None of these

8. To use the word processor to create a file once you have entered
    the computer

    [1]   WP/NAME/LOG
    [2]   LOG/WP/NAME
    [3]   LOG/WP/OF
    [4]   LOG/WP/NAME/OF
    [5]   None of these

5.   Coded instructions (3)

Checking databases

To enter the computer, type	LOG/SYS
To check database one, type	DBO
To check database two, type	DBT
To check database three, type	DBT/R
To delete a file from database, type	ND/followed by the code of the appropriate database
To create a file in the database, type	CF/followed by the database code

Which code should be used for the following?

1. To delete a file from database three (assume you have already entered the computer)

    [1]   DBT/R
    [2]   ND/LOG/DBT/R
    [3]   ND/DBT/R
    [4]   ND/DBO
    [5]   None of these

2. To check database two (assume you have already entered the computer)

    [1]   DBT
    [2]   DBO
    [3]   DBT/R
    [4]   DBO/T/R
    [5]   None of these

3. To enter the computer and check database one

    [1]   DBO
    [2]   LOG/SYS/DBO
    [3]   LOG/SYS/DBT/R
    [4]   DBT/R/O
    [5]   None of these

4. To create a file in database two (assume you have already entered the computer)

    [1]   LOG/SYS/CF/DBT
    [2]   CF/DBO/T
    [3]   CF/DBT
    [4]   ND/DBT
    [5]   None of these

5. To enter the computer and create a file in database three

    [1]   CF/DBT/R
    [2]   CF/DBT
    [3]   ND/DBT/R
    [4]   ND/DBT
    [5]   None of these

6. To enter the computer and delete a file in database one

    [1]   ND/DBO
    [2]   LOG/SYS/ND/DBO
    [3]   LOG/SYS/ND/DBT
    [4]   LOG/SYS/ND/DBT/R
    [5]   None of these

7. To enter the computer

    [1]   LOG/SYS/DBO
    [2]   LOG/SYS
    [3]   LOG/ON/SYS
    [4]   LOG/ON/DU/DE
    [5]   None of these

8. To create a file in database two and then delete a file in database one (assume you have already entered the computer)

    [1]   CF/DBO & CF/DBT
    [2]   CF/DBT & CF/DBO
    [3]   CF/DBT & ND/DBT
    [4]   CF/DBT & ND/DBO
    [5]   None of these

9. To enter the computer and check database three and then create a file in database two

    [1]   LOG/SYS/DBT/R & CF/DBO
    [2]   LOG/SYS/DBT/R & CF/DBT
    [3]   LOG/SYS/DBT/R & CF/DBT/R
    [4]   DBT/R & CF/DBT
    [5]   None of these

10. To check database one, then create a file in database two and finally delete a file in database three (assume you have already logged on)

    [1]   DBO & CF/DBT & ND/DBT/R
    [2]   CF/DBO & DBO & ND/DBT/R
    [3]   DBO & ND/DBT & CF/DBT/R
    [4]   DBO/DBO/CF/DBT/RO/NG
    [5]   None of these

6. Sequencing

In this exercise you have to put a list of events in a logical order. Under each list of events there are a number of boxes in which you are to put the numbers of the events in their logical order.

Example: Creating a file in a word processor

1. Load program 2. Switch on computer
3. Type 4. Switch off computer 5. Save file

Now try these:

A. Going to work

1. Get on train 2. Get up 3. Go to platform
4. Get off train 5. Arrive at other end 6. Leave home
7. Get to station

B.   Changing a wheel of a car
1.   Put on spare wheel   2. Undo the bolts
3.   Remove old wheel   4. Tighten bolts

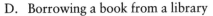

C.   Using a cash dispenser machine
1.   Input amount of money required
2.   Type in correct number
3.   Remove card and money
4.   Insert card

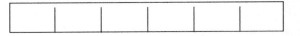

D.   Borrowing a book from a library
1.   Take the book to the librarian
2.   Locate the appropriate book case
3.   Note the index code
4.   Locate the appropriate section of the library
5.   Consult the book location index
6.   Locate the book

E.   Solving a problem
1.   Apply the solution. 2. Identify the problem
3.   Select the best solution
4.   Suggest as many solutions as possible

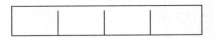

F. Constructing a valid argument 1
　　1. Conclusion: Mary is a European
　　2. Germans are also Europeans
　　3. Mary is a German

G. Constructing a valid argument 2
　　1. Conclusion: Peter is not a European
　　2. Peter says he is an American subject
　　3. If he said he is American that means he cannot be European
　　4. Is Peter European?

H. Tom is a tall person but he is not taller than Jeff. Tom is taller than both George and Ray. Jeff is shorter than Chris. Write the first letter of the tallest person's name.

I. Raheel is Naseem's son. Naseem has a brother called Khalid. The two brothers' father has a daughter, Gazala, who is older than Khalid but younger than Naseem. What is the relationship between Raheel and Gazala?

J. A car is being driven due north. After five miles it turns 180 degrees. Write the first letter of the direction in which the car is now travelling.

Further examples of this type of question can be found in the Kogan Page titles, *How to Pass Verbal Reasoning Tests, How to Pass the Civil Service Qualifying Tests* and *How to Pass Computer Selection Tests.*

Answers and explanations

Chapter 4.   Some of the most common types of test

1.   Verbal tests that measure comprehension (page 23)

A.   Swapping words

First example   'test' and 'hard'
Second example   'limit' and 'virtually'

B.   Finding missing words
B

C.   Locating words that mean the same or the opposite
First example   C
Second example B

2.   Tests of grammar and punctuation (page 25)

A.   Choosing from a number of sentences
First example   (c)
Second example (a)

B.   Choosing from pairs of words

First example   D
Second example D

3.   Spelling tests (page 28)

Example 1
You should have underlined:
sincerely, foreign, immediate, merchandise, shampoo

Example 2
You should have written out the following words:
balance, beautify, correlate, disease

Example 3
Question 1   1, 18, 20
Question 2   21, 5, 19

4.   Tests of logical thinking (page 30)

A.   Following instructions

Example 1   B
Example 2   C

B.   Relationships between numbers and statements

Example 1   15. Each number is 4 greater than the previous one.
Example 2   (d) Stoke on Trent (all the others are islands)
Example 3   16. All the others can be divided by 5.
Example 4   C. All the others have two lines in the box.

5.   Numerical tests (page 33)

A.   The four rules

1.   1040327
2.   370818
3.   2
4.   410
5.   1319396
6.   20

B.   Practical numerical problems

Example 1   £15
Example 2   £73.52
Example 3   £25
Example 4   £21

C.   Estimating/approximating

Example 1   D
Example 2   A

D.   Percentages and fractions

Example 1 $1^5/_{12}$
Example 2   A
Example 3   £6.75
Example 4   £752
Example 5   £91.20
Example 6   B

6.   Tests of clerical and computing skills (page 39)

A.   Flow diagrams

2

B.   Sequencing

4, 5, 2, 3, 1

C.   Coded instructions

1.   OF
2.   DFESC
3.   OFSPSF

D. Checking computer data

1	Land Scales Ltd	9 Lanca Place	N	Lancaster Gate	N	ES2 5HJ	Y
2	Fox Associates	143 West Side	Y	Ealing	Y	5HJ 6TT	Y
3	Collers Building	68 Cambridge Street	N	Queens Way	Y	3DD 5TG	N
4	Top Creation	11 Gorge Road	Y	Plaistow	N	9NN 4RF	Y
5	Victoria Pack Systems	34a Major Street	N	Great Harwood	Y	2DE 6VC	N
6	Municipal Supplies	22 Warehouse Road	Y	Small Health	Y	8MN 6AS	N
7	Barton Hotel	78 Baker Street	N	Uxbrige	Y	12DD 5TT	N
8	Save Finances	53 Church Yard Close	N	Sherman	Y	7FC 4DX	Y
9	Longsdale LTD	2 Burton Street	N	Hackney	Y	E5 2CD	Y
10	Western Electronic	10 Resister Road	N	EastHam	N	E9 4RF	N
11	New Technology	13 Forth Avenue	N	Manor Park	N	E12 5NT	Y
12	Net Surfing Cafe	20 Cyber Street	Y	Compton	Y	CB13 7FG	Y
13	Super Robotics Plc	145 Well Street	N	High Grove	N	HG8 2WL	Y
14	Info Tech Ltd	1 New Lane	Y	Hertfordshire	Y	NW3 25A	N
15	Printers Printers	2 Print Street	N	Printington	Y	PTS 2PR	N

Chapter 5.   Practice material

Verbal tests (pages 46–121)

1.   The same meaning or the opposite (page 46)

	Opposites	*Same*
store	waste	stockpile
wrong	right	mistaken
question	answer	enquire
measure	guess-work	gauge
problem	solution	obstacle
obscure	transparent	conceal
synthetic	natural	man-made
vertical	horizontal	upright
repair	neglect	recondition
strengthen	weaken	augment

1.   pedalo
2.   ability
3.   brawl
4.   mud
5.   short

2.   Sound alike/look alike words (page 49)

Exercise 1
1.   bore, boar
2.   specific, Pacific
3.   morning, mourning
4.   principle, principal
5.   waist, waste
6.   there, their

Exercise 2
1.   knew   5. few
2.   too   6. draft
3.   guerrillas   7. quiet
4.   rap   8. rites

9. alms	18. patients
10. lead	19. through
11. affecting	20. seat
12. whether	21. heard
13. accepted	22. hoarse
14. feat	23. mail
15. there	24. scene
16. cite	25. except
17. off	26. their

3.   Choosing the right word (page 53)

1. there
2. eaten
3. has
4. as though
5. nor
6. that
7. were
8. I

4.   Timed exercise – choosing the right word (page 54)

1. knew	leaving
2. you	have
3. able	woman
4. weather	fine
5. flew	across
6. agree	differ
7. tired	colour
8. column	rows
9. program	used
10. centre	manager

5.   Choosing the right sentence (page 56)

1. B
2. A
3. A
4. A
5. C

6.   Timed exercise – choosing the right sentence (page 59)
   1. C
   2. B
   3. B
   4. C
   5. A
   6. D
   7. D
   8. C
   9. E
  10. D

7.   Plural words (page 62)
   1. C
   2. D
   3. B
   4. B
   5. B
   6. E
   7. D
   8. A
   9. E
  10. D
  11. D
  12. D
  13. A
  14. B
  15. A
  16. B
  17. C
  18. A
  19. B
  20. D
  21. C
  22. B
  23. A

24. A
25. B
26. B
27. B
28. A
29. B
30. A
31. E
32. B
33. C
34. B
35. E

8. Spelling (page 67)

1.	67	17	19	48
2.	27	7		
3.	41	34		
4.	12	21	46	
5.	15	19		
6.	28	56	73	55
7.	5	20	30	74
8.	67	22	65	24

9. Timed spelling (page 71)

1.	8	46	47	
2.	38	72	7	58
3.	14	32	11	71
4.	18	24		
5.	75	41	43	
6.	5	13	65	29
7.	55	12	6	56
8.	57	62	59	
9.	48	64	39	73
10.	54	74	67	

10.   Reading for information (page 76)

1. False
2. False
3. True
4. True
5. False
6. False
7. False
8. False
9. True

A different style of reading for information question

Q1 Answer: Cannot tell
Explanation: The passage does not say which of the inner planets is closest to the sun.

Q2 Answer: True
Explanation: The passage states that all the outer planets have moons.

Q3 Answer: False
Explanation: The passage states that there are five, the four large gaseous planets and Pluto.

Q4 Answer: False
Explanation: Mars is described as one of the inner planets while Jupiter is described as one of the outer planets. From this it can be inferred that Jupiter is further from the sun than Mars.

Q5 Answer: True
Explanation: The passage states that the number of sufferers from high blood pressure is forecast to rise further both in developed and developing countries.

Q6 Answer: Cannot tell
Explanation: The passage states that it is estimated that 1 billion people suffer from high blood pressure but the passage does not indicate how many will die as a result of suffering this condition.

Q7 Answer: False
Explanation: The passage states ways in which it can be reduced.

Q8 Answer: Cannot tell
Explanation: The passage does not provide information on this point.

Q9 Answer: False
Explanation: The passage states that the moon provides twice the gravitation pull of the sun but this still means that the sun's gravitational force contributes to the tidal effect.

Q10 Answer: Cannot tell
Explanation: The locations of the occurrences are not detailed in the passages.

Q11 Answer: Cannot tell
Explanation: The passage makes no comment on this issue.

Q12 Answer: True
Explanation: The passage states that the second bulge is caused this way.

Q13 Answer: True
Explanation: The passage states that the medieval period lasted from 1000 to 1500, which is 500 years.

Q14 Answer: True
Explanation: The passage states that most people lived in the countryside.

Q15 Answer: Cannot tell
Explanation: The passage does not provide any information on the effect of a bad harvest.

Q16 Answer: False
Explanation: The passage states that the Dark Ages preceded the medieval period, which means the Dark Ages were before the medieval period.

Q17 Answer: False
Explanation: The passage states that the heating effect might cause harm to our brains but it does not say that it could warm brain tissue.

Q18 Answer: True
Explanation: The passage states that mobile phones work by transmitting and receiving radio waves and that these waves create electromagnetic fields.

Q19 Answer: True
Explanation: The passage states that they are a part of the spectrum along with visible light microwaves and x rays.

Q20 Answer: Cannot tell
Explanation: The passage provides no information on the susceptibility of children.

Q21 Answer: Cannot tell
Explanation: The passage provides no information on the accuracy of forecasts made from these test scores.

Q22 Answer: False
Explanation: The passage does not state this.

Q23 Answer: True
Explanation: As adults they had gone on to realise average scores.

Q24 Answer: Cannot tell
Explanation: The passage provides no explanation for the differences in the groups' performances.

Q25 Answer: True
Explanation: Immigration and emigration affect the population of particular areas but not the world population as a whole.

Q26 Answer: False
Explanation: The passage states that the population is determined by the balance between birth and death rates and a higher birth rate may not result in a higher world population if the death rate also increases.

Q27 Answer: Cannot tell
Explanation: The passage provides no information on the future expected growth or decline of the world's population.

Q28 Answer: False
Explanation: Higher immigration into an area will lead the population to increase not decrease.

Q29 Answer: False
Explanation: The passage does not state anything about the languages spoken by Americans.

Q30 Answer: False
Explanation: The passage states that America's wealth is also derived from other factors.

Q31 Answer: Cannot tell
Explanation: While we all know this is true it is not stated in the passage so you must conclude that we cannot tell.

Q32 Answer: True
Explanation: America is the third most populous nation with 281 million people so the next most populous must have a population smaller than this.

Q33 Answer: True
Explanation: The passage states that to the south of the Azores lie
Madeira and the Canaries.

Q34 Answer: Cannot tell
Explanation: The passage does not say whether or not the Azores are
a developed holiday destination.

Q35 Answer: False
Explanation: St Helena is described as further south of the Cape
Verde.

Q36 Answer: True
Explanation: The passage states that the Cape Verde and all islands
south are much quieter.

Q37 Answer: Cannot tell
Explanation: The passage does not indicate what might be
proportionate fines for particular offences.

Q38 Answer: False
Explanation: They prefer a system where the level of fine is
proportionate to the seriousness of the crime.

Q39 Answer: True
Explanation: Provided that they were in the same income bracket.

Q40 Answer: False
Explanation: The passage states that commentators concluded that
the public prefer a system where a fine acts as a deterrent and for this
to happen the person fined should to some extent struggle to pay it.
For this to happen the fine must still bear some relationship to the
offender's income.

11.   Alphabetical order (page 96)

Arranging words – Example 1
1.   Acrobat
2.   Gangster
3.   Heiress
4.   Kidnap
5.   Orator
6.   Puff-adder
7.   Reptile
8.   Sorrow

Arranging words – Example 2
1.   Fabric
2.   Faithful
3.   Farmyard
4.   Feather
5.   February
6.   Fixer
7.   Florida
8.   Foliage

Rearranging letters
1.   achirty
2.   iloqru
3.   acginor
4.   aehmst
5.   hip
6.   deny
7.   lot
8.   bmr

Timed exercise

Name	File Number	Name	File Number
Young	18	Warner	18
Bayard	3	Carrington	5
Harvey	9	Christie	5
Fisher	8	Tooling	16
Skinner	15	Arnold	2
Bishop	3	Hood	9
Adler	1	Dell	7

12. Comparisons 1 (page 100)

1. B   2. C   3. A   4. C   5. C   6. B   7. B   8. B
9. B   10. B

Comparisons 2 (page 101)

1. B   2. C   3. A   4. C   5. A   6. B   7. C

13. Odd-one-out (page 102)

1. A   2. D   3. D   4. E   5. E   6. C   7. E   8. D
9. C   10. C   11. A   12. E

14. Opposites (page 102)

1. B   2. B   3. C   4. B   5. C   6. B   7. A   8. B
9. B   10. C

15. Similar sounding words (page 103)

Exercise 1

1. cite/site	2. coarse	3. draught
4. brooch	5. knew	6. damn
7. whether	8. dew	9. male
10. dye	11. gail/gayle	12. suite
13. right/wright	14. too/two	15. red
16. tale	17. buy/by	18. won

19. waive	20. four/fore	21. knead
22. flour	23. breech	24. soul
25. scene	26. hare	27. son
28. herd	29. seam	30. hart

Exercise 2

1. fete	2. here	3. grate
4. whole	5. know	6. mane
7. board	8. ail	9. bald
10. knight	11. bear	12. nit
13. break	14. minor	15. bred
16. navel	17. scent	18. nun
19. meat	20. oar/ore	21. off
22. piece	23. peal	24. pear
25. peak	26. plait	27. poll
28. pool	29. pore	30. reign/rein
31. prey	32. programme	33. purl
34. quay	35. wrest	36. wrap
37. wreak	38. wring	39. wry
40. shoo		

17.   Homophones (page 105)

1. hymn	2. site/cite	3. bald	4. seam
5. bean	6. wring	7. write/wright	8. knight
9. fort	10. through	11. bough	12. wrung
13. pane	14. weight	15. break	16. grate
17. knew	18. know	19. sea	20. wear

18.   More homophones (page 106)

1. hear	2. bear	3. fare	4. hare
5. tee	6. pair	7. deer	8. four/fore
9. bait	10. fete	11. bail	12. sail
13. ail	14. tail	15. veil	16. wail
17. witch	18. pail	19. wore	20. son

19.   Homophones again (page 107)

1. mail	2. to/too	3. so	4. whole
5. flair	6. doe	7. quay	8. plane
9. cheque	10. fir	11. knot	12. cue
13. leek	14. feat	15. beet	16. boar
17. board	18. ewe	19. suite	20. tyre

20.   Synonyms (page 108)

1	Nearby	Close		11	Brawl	Fight
2	Climb	Ascend		12	Foe	Enemy
3	Absolute	Complete		13	Idea	Concept
4	Foreign	Alien		14	Kidnap	Abduct
5	Abuse	Misuse		15	Alike	Similar
6	Distant	Far		16	Behind	Enemy
7	Ocean	Sea		17	Benefit	Advantage
8	Arbiter	Judge		18	Garbage	Rubbish
9	Mate	Friend		19	Outlaw	Bandit
10	Aroma	Fragrance		20	Sound	Audio

21.   More synonyms (page 109)

1	Empty	Blank		11	Border	Boundary
2	Wound	Gash		12	Pester	Bother
3	Least	Smallest		13	Fragile	Brittle
4	Grab	Seize		14	Inferior	Crummy
5	Channel	Groove		15	Lavatory	Latrine
6	Insect	Bug		16	Oppose	Counter
7	Refuse	Garbage		17	Sneer	Fleer
8	Jail	Gaol		18	Shut	Close
9	Sham	Bogus		19	Gift	Present
10	Drum	Bongo		20	Cheese	Curd

1	Rude	Insolent		11	Insane	Mad
2	Sailor	Mariner		12	Smell	Odour
3	Foe	Enemy		13	Dampness	Moisture
4	Unite	Join		14	Forbid	Prohibit
5	Fable	Myth		15	Wide	Broad
6	Sharp	Acute		16	Control	Curb
7	Weariness	Fatigue		17	Rough	Coarse
8	Feeble	Weak		18	Hide	Conceal
9	Round	Circular		19	Inside	Interior
10	Dwelling	Abode		20	Hard	Difficult

1	Peaceful	Tranquil		11	Anger	Wrath
2	Clear	Transparent		12	Quick	Rapid
3	Riches	Wealth		13	Purchase	Buy
4	Strict	Stern		14	Pointless	Futile
5	Horse	Steed		15	Cure	Remedy
6	Slim	Slender		16	Show	Reveal
7	Position	Rank		17	Strong	Sturdy
8	Empty	Vacant		18	Yield	Surrender
9	Annually	Yearly		19	Smooth	Sleek
10	Defeat	Vanquish		20	Hang	Suspend

22. Antonyms (page 112)

1. Flexible   Rigid (6)
2. Solid   Liquid (9)
3. Shiny   Dull (4)
4. Enemy   Friend (19)
5. High   Low (8)
6. Above   Below (16)
7. Back   Front (12)
8. Left   Right (14)
9. Shut   Open (17)
10. Bad   Good (10)

23.   More antonyms (page 113)

1. Empty   Full (6)
2. Last   First (17)
3. Fluid   Solid (4)
4. Increment   Decrease (12)
5. Loose   Fixed (8)
6. Motivate   Discourage (11)
7. Extract   Replace (7)
8. Plural   Singular (13)
9. Pliable   Rigid (16)
10. Plenty   Scarce (19)

24.   Creating compound words (page 114)

1. Sun	Day	2. He	Art
3. Motor	Car	4. Flip	Side
5. After	Noon	6. Allow	Able
7. Alpha	Bet	8. Amalgam	Ate
9. Anti	Body	10. Anti	Christ
11. Anti	Social	12. Audio	Meter
13. Auto	Graph	14. Auto	Mate
15. Back	Hand	16. Back	Ache
17. Back	Ward	18. Bag	Pipe
19. High	Land	20. Rail	Way
21. Base	Ball	22. Bat	Ten
23. Be	Come	24 Bed	Clothes
25. Bed	Pan		

25.   More compound words (page 115)

1. Blind	Date	2. Block	Age
3. Bother	Some	4. Top	Less
5. Blind	Spot	6. Bread	Crumb
7. Break	Fast	8. Blind	Fold
9. Bride	Groom	10. Brief	Case
11. Brute	Force	12. Break	Able
13. Chain	Saw	14. Chair	Man
15. Chamber	Maid	16. Brides	Maid

17. Colour	Blind	18. Common	Wealth
19. Copy	Right	20. Corn	Wall
21. Counter	Foil	22. Crash	Land
23. Counter	Balance	24. Counter	Act
25. Table	Spoon		

26.   Compound words again (page 116)

1. Coat	Hanger	2. Gear	Stick
3. Import	Ant	4 Home	Work
5. Honey	Comb	6. Hour	Glass
7. Man	Kind	8. Dead	Line
9. Ice	Cream	10. Honey	Moon
11. Honey	Pot	12. Bed	Linen
13. Beet	Root	14. Be	Hold
15. Birth	Day	16. Black	Head
17. Church	Warden	18. Class	Less
19. Cloak	Room	20. Grand	Father
21. Coast	Guard	22. Fat	Her
23. Game	Keeper	24 Plat	Form
25. Sat	Urn		

27.   Four-minute compound words (page 117)

1. Broad	Cast	2. Brother	Hood
3. Bump	Kin	4. Bus	King
5. Cap	Able	6. Care	Less
7. Car	Rot	8. Check	Mate
9. Car	Ton	10. Broad	Way
11. Common	Place	12. Complain	Ant
13. Gentle	Man	14. Gate	Way
15. For	Given	16. Fox	Hound
17. Fond	Ant	18. Foot	Steps
19. Eye	Brow	20. Feat	Her
21. Fabric	Ate	22. Friend	Ship
23. Foot	Path	24. Game	Keeper
25. Cool	Ant		

28.   Three-minute compound words (page 118)

1. Fruit	Less	2. Gain	Fully
3. For	Ward	4. Four	Some
5. Frame	Work	6. Land	Mark
7. Eye	Lid	8. Fare	Well
9. Cot	Ton	10. Feed	Back
11. For	Tune	12. Gate	Crash
13. Fly	Wheel	14. God	Son
15. For	Age	16. Flash	Back
17. Dart	Mouth	18. Eye	Sight
19. Under	Mine	20. Count	Less
21. Good	Will	22. Grand	Stand
23. Fly	Over	24. Counter	Part
25. Foot	Hold		

29.   Analogies (page 119)

1. (b) fly	2. (c) pup	3. (d) couple	4. (b) fish
5. (a) daughter	6. (b) December	7. (c) orange	8. (c) wires
9. (d) flock	10. (a) east	11. (b) commence	12. (a) foot
13. (b) peruse	14. (a) museum	15. (a) automobile	16. (d) pride
17. (b) plague	18. (c) troop	19. (a) school	20. (b) troupe
21. (c) library	22. (b) leap	23. (c) mass	24. (b) two
25. (c) elver			

Numerical tests (pages 121–53)

1.   The four rules, percentages and fractions (page 122)

Addition

1. 3	2. 9	3. 7	4. 10	5. 11
6. 18	7. 24	8. 27	9. 69	10. 46
11. 0	12. 150	13. 2.1	14. 3	15. 20.5
16. 4.1	17. 40	18. 305	19. 1640	20. 136
21. 1010	22. 4.6	23. 1	24. 480	25. 37
26. 193	27. 200	28. 7	29. 1	30. 6.2

Subtraction

1. 5
2. 3
3. 16
4. 42
5. 2
6. 2.36
7. 6407
8. 5182
9. 29090
10. 21289
11. 322799
12. 5714.08
13. 461.28
14. 2476.38
15. 5756.60
16. 39517
17. 46287.97
18. 274.965

Multiplication

1. 29315
2. 3800
3. 4911
4. 9944
5. 2583
6. 85335
7. 99756
8. 660850
9. 524988395
10. 52813950
11. 193897.60
12. 23121.60
13. 7300088.10

Division

1. 3
2. 6
3. 7
4. 4
5. 190
6. 45
7. 65
8. 1020
9. 477
10. 13.2
11. 11.5
12. 12.3

Timed division

1. 224
2. 10.5
3. 25.3

Percentages

1. 25
2. 21
3. 10
4. 22.5
5. 750
6. 1664
7. 55%
8. 47%
9. 675
10. 87
11. 5%
12. 865
13. 3.96
14. 85
15. 40

Fractions
1. 1
2. 4
3. ½
4. 10
5. 5
6. 8
7. 14
8. 15
9. 20
10. 25
11. $^{11}/_{12}$
12. $2^{1}/_{3}$
13. 4½
14. $34^{1}/_{8}$
15. $3^{1}/_{12}$
16. 160
17. 25

2.   Approximating (pages 127–46)

Rounding off numbers (1)

1. 100
2. 10
3. 2
4. 9
5. 8
6. 500
7. 115
8. 6
9. 3
10. 6
11. 2
12. 8
13. 6
14. 8
15. 45

Rounding off numbers (2)

1. 20% of 700
2. 100% of 50
3. 50% of 60
4. 20% of 1000
5. 50% of 200
6. 20% of 100
7. 200% of 100
8. 10% of 900
9. 50% of 800
10. 40% of 80
11. 10% of 40
12. 5% of 50
13. 5% of 100
14. 120% of 1000
15. 10% of 700

Rounding off numbers (3)

1. 15
2. 552
3. 8
4. 300
5. 200
6. 14000
7. 3500
8. 2000
9. 1
10. 2
11. 17
12. 800
13. 600
14. 5
15. 5

Addition

1. 448.49
2. 6232
3. 998
4. 7197.6
5. 100.916
6. 150
7. 506
8. 1230
9. 15100
10. 7430

Subtraction

1. 122
2. 27
3. 1.92
4. 2488
5. 10.22
6. 463
7. 4795
8. 229
9. 9587.88
10. 73.85

Multiplication

1. 1475
2. 14820
3. 125
4. 1650
5. 2500
6. 165
7. 10000
8. 30000
9. 99.99
10. 49.95

Division

1. 8.2
2. 22
3. 1.8
4. 110
5. 990

Percentages

1. 50
2. 120
3. 329.67
4. 367.01
5. 250
6. 201.84
7. 17.28
8. 72
9. 2090
10. 450

Fractions

1. 13¾
2. 8
3. 60
4. 31
5. 2$^{1}/_{12}$

Mixed

1. 99	2. 80	3. 9.31	4. 162	5. 43.88
6. 75.4	7. 142.45	8. 70.41	9. 1233	10. 1111
11. 5472	12. 5			

More percentages and some essential ratios

Q1
Answer: 50%
Explanation: $100 \div 2 = 50 \times 1 = 50$

Q2
Answer: 25%
Explanation: $100 \div 4 = 25 \times 1 = 25$

Q3
Answer: 33.3%
Explanation: $100 \div 3 = 33.3 \times 1 = 33.3$

Q4
Answer: 20%
Explanation: $100 \div 5 = 20 \times 1 = 20$

Q5
Answer: 12.5%
Explanation: $100 \div 8 = 12.5 \times 1 = 12.5$

Q6
Answer: 6.25%
Explanation: $100 \div 16 = 6.25 \times 1 = 6.25$

Q7
Answer: 8.3%
Explanation: $100 \div 12 = 8.3 \times 1 = 8.3$

Q8
Answer: 11.1%
Explanation: $100 \div 9 = 11.1 \times 1 = 11.1$

Q9
Answer: 66.6%
Explanation: $100 \div 3 = 33.3 \times 2 = 66.6$

Q10
Answer: 60%
Explanation: $100 \div 5 = 20 \times 3 = 60$

Q11
Answer: 37.5%
Explanation: $100 \div 16 = 6.25 \times 6 = 37.5$

Q12
Answer: 62.5%
Explanation: $100 \div 8 = 12.5 \times 5 = 62.5$

Changing between decimals and percentages

Q1
Answer: 50%
Explanation: $0.5 \times 100 = 50$

Q2
Answer: 20%
Explanation: $0.2 \times 100 = 20$

Q3
Answer: 60%
Explanation: $0.6 \times 100 = 60$

Q4
Answer: 40%
Explanation: $0.4 \times 100 = 40$

Q5
Answer: 35%
Explanation: $0.35 \times 100 = 35$

Q6
Answer: 72%
Explanation: $0.72 \times 100 = 72$

Q7
Answer: 42.5%
Explanation: $0.425 \times 100 = 42.5$

Q8
Answer: 33.3%
Explanation: $0.333 \times 100 = 33.3$

Q9
Answer: 53.25%
Explanation: $0.5325 \times 100 = 53.25$

Q10
Answer: 0.25
Explanation: $25 \div 100 = 0.25$

Q11
Answer: 0.9
Explanation: $90 \div 100 = 0.9$

Q12
Answer: 0.05
Explanation: $5 \div 100 = 0.05$

Q13
Answer: 0.15
Explanation: $15 \div 100 = 0.15$

Q14
Answer: 0.024
Explanation: $2.4 \div 100 = 0.024$

Q15
Answer: 0.006
Explanation: $0.6 \div 100 = 0.006$

A value expressed as a percentage of another

Q1
Answer: 30%
Explanation: $15 \div 50 = 0.3 \times 100 = 30$

Q2
Answer: 12%
Explanation: $3 \div 25 = 0.12 \times 100 = 12$

Q3
Answer: 12.5%
Explanation: $5 \div 40 = 0.125 \times 100 = 12.5$

Q4
Answer: 20%
Explanation: $1 \div 5 = 0.2 \times 100 = 20$

Q5
Answer: 8%
Explanation: $6 \div 75 = 0.08 \times 100 = 8$

Q6
Answer: 80%
Explanation: $10 \div 12.5 = 0.8 \times 100 = 80$

Q7
Answer: 12.5%
Explanation: $2 \div 16 = 0.125 \times 100 = 12.5$

Q8
Answer: 5%
Explanation: $4 \div 8 = 0.05 \times 100 = 5$

Q9
Answer: 30%
Explanation: $12 \div 40 = 0.3 \times 100 = 30$

Q10
Answer: 40%
Explanation: $28 \div 70 = 0.4 \times 100 = 40$

Finding percentages of quantities

Q1
Answer: £32
Explanation: $0.4 \times 80 = 32$

Q2
Answer: 45 minutes
Explanation: Convert the hours into minutes, $3 \times 60 = 180$, $0.25 \times 180 = 45$

Q3
Answer: 6 metres
Explanation: $0.15 \times 40 = 6$

Q4
Answer: £1.80
Explanation: $0.2 \times 9 = 1.8$

Q5
Answer: 600cm
Explanation: $0.05 \times 12 = 0.6$

Q6
Answer: 1 hour and 12 minutes
Explanation: 720 minutes $\times 0.1 = 72 = 1$ hour and 12 minutes

Q7
Answer: £78
Explanation: $0.15 \times 520 = 78$

Q8
Answer: 27 minutes
Explanation: 90 minutes $\times 0.3 = 27$

Q9
Answer: 3m, 660cm
Explanation: $0.2 \times 18.3 = 3.66$

Q10
Answer: 52 minutes and 30 seconds
Explanation: $5 \times 60 = 300$ minutes, $300 \times 0.175 = 52.5 = 52$ minutes and 30 seconds

Percentage increase

Q1
Answer: 50%
Explanation: 10 (the increase) $\div 20 = 0.5 \times 100 = 50$

Q2
Answer: 20%
Explanation: $8 \div 40 = 0.2 \times 100 = 20$

Q3
Answer: 25%
Explanation: $6 \div 24 = 0.25 \times 100 = 25$

Q4
Answer: 40%
Explanation: $32 \div 80 = 0.4 \times 100 = 40$

Q5
Answer: 60%
Explanation: $6.6 \div 11 = 0.6 \times 100 = 60$

Q6
Answer: 30%
Explanation: $7.5 \div 25 = 0.3 \times 100 = 30$

Q7
Answer: 8%
Explanation: $7.2 \div 90 = 0.08 \times 100 = 8$

Q8
Answer: 12.5%
Explanation: $1 \div 8 = 0.0125 \times 100 = 12.5$

Q9
Answer: 4%
Explanation: $4.8 \div 120 = 0.04 \times 100 = 4$

Q10
Answer: 60%
Explanation: $21.6 \div 36 = 0.6 \times 100 = 60$

Percentage decrease
Q1
Answer: 5%
Explanation: $5 \div 100 = 0.05 \times 100 = 5$

Q2
Answer: 16%
Explanation: $8 \div 50 = 0.16 \times 100 = 16$

Q3
Answer: 24%
Explanation: $18 \div 75 = 0.24 \times 100 = 24$

Q4
Answer: 45%
Explanation: $36 \div 80 = 0.45 \times 100 = 45$

Q5
Answer: 60%
Explanation: $72 \div 120 = 0.6 \times 100 = 60$

Q6
Answer: 75%
Explanation: $6 \div 8 = 0.75 \times 100 = 75$

Q7
Answer: 90%
Explanation: $81 \div 90 = 0.9 \times 100 = 90$

Q8
Answer: 30%
Explanation: $7.5 \div 25 = 0.3 \times 100 = 30$

Q9
Answer: 12%
Explanation: $3.6 \div 30 = 0.12 \times 100 = 12$

Q10
Answer: 22%
Explanation: $14.3 \div 65 = 0.22 \times 100 = 22$

Percentage profit or loss

Q1
Answer: 20% profit
Explanation: $2 \div 10 = 0.2 \times 100 = 20$

Q2
Answer: 20% loss
Explanation: $8 \div 40 = 0.2 \times 100 = 20$

Q3
Answer: 40% profit
Explanation: $20 \div 50 = 0.4 \times 100 = 40$

Q4
Answer: 12.5% loss
Explanation: $1 \div 8 = 0.125 \times 100 = 12.5$

Q5
Answer: 30% profit
Explanation: $7.5 \div 25 = 0.3 \times 100 = 30$

Q6
Answer: 80% loss
Explanation: $9.6 \div 12 = 0.8 \times 100 = 80$

Q7
Answer: 15% profit
Explanation: $0.75 \div 5 = 0.15 \times 100 = 15$

Q8
Answer: 70% loss
Explanation: $31.5 \div 45 = 0.7 \times 100 = 70$

Q9
Answer: 60% profit
Explanation: $42 \div 70 = 0.6 \times 100 = 60$

Q10
Answer: 6% loss
Explanation: $0.39 \div 65 = 0.06 \times 100 = 6$

Ratios

Q1
Answer: 80 : 20
Explanation: $4 + 1 = 5, 100 \div 5 = 20, 4 \times 20 = 80, 1 \times 20 = 20$

Q2
Answer: 21 : 28
Explanation: $3 + 4 = 7, 49 \div 7 = 7, 3 \times 7 = 21, 4 \times 7 = 28$

Q3
Answer: 6 : 30
Explanation: $1 + 5 = 6, 36 \div 6 = 6, 1 \times 6 = 6, 5 \times 6 = 30$

Q4
Answer: 45 : 27
Explanation: $5 + 3 = 8, 72 \div 8 = 9, 5 \times 9 = 45, 3 \times 9 = 27$

Q5
Answer: 33 : 22
Explanation: $3 + 2 = 5, 55 \div 5 = 11, 3 \times 11 = 33, 2 \times 11 = 22$

Q6
Answer: 13 : 91 : 26
Explanation: $1 + 7 + 2 = 10, 130 \div 10 = 13, 1 \times 13 = 13, 7 \times 13 = 91,$
$2 \times 13 = 26$

Q7
Answer: 24 : 16 : 12
Explanation: $6 + 4 + 3 = 13, 52 \div 13 = 4, 6 \times 4 = 24, 4 \times 4 = 16, 3 \times 4$
$= 12$

Q8
Answer: 17.5 : 7.5 : 30
Explanation: $7 + 3 + 12 = 22, 55 \div 22 = 2.5, 7 \times 2.5 = 17.5, 3 \times 2.5 =$
$7.5, 12 \times 2.5 = 30$

Q9
Answer: 3.5 : 14: 10.5
Explanation: $1 + 4 + 3 = 8, 28 \div 8 = 3.5, 1 \times 3.5 = 3.5, 4 \times 3.5 = 14, 3$
$\times 3.5 = 10.5.$

Q10
Answer: 16.5 : 27.5: 22
Explanation: $3 + 5 + 4 = 11, 60.5 \div 11 = 5.5, 3 \times 5.5 = 16.5, 5 \times 5.5$
$27.5, 4 \times 5.5 = 22$

3.   Practical numerical problems (pages 146–53)

1. £12.00
2. £55.66
3. 22½ hours
4. 5250 people
5. £176.25
6. £572
7. £9750

8. £12,000
9. £13
10. (a) £1665
    (b) £555
11. £37.50
12. £37.50
13. £25
14. £300.88

Timed practical numerical problems

1. £10.70
2. £15.40
3. 85.6 pence

Foreign currency exchange rates

1. D (130)
2. E (None of these)
3. C (12.60)
4. C (300)
5. B (6500)
6. D (110)
7. D (1250, 375, 625,000)
8. B (337.78)
9. C (4722.22)
10. B (3600)

Clerical tests (pages 154–94)

1. Coded instructions (page 154)

Exercise 1

1. Down the launderette
2. Watching the news on TV
3. 12.00
4. Paying the milk bill
5. 12.00
6. 9 am

Exercise 2

1. udyne	lippgai	nitco	modod
2. Tratma	nitco	udyne	lippgai
3. ranch	udyne	modod	lippgai

Into English

1. Fido the dog
2. Is Fido black?
3. Is the dog Fido?

Exercise 3

1. D
2. B
3. D

Timed coded instructions exercise

1. D
2. D
3. B
4. D
5. D

Exercise 4

1. 15 years
2. 1hr and 3 min (63 min)
3. 3.6 kg (3600 grams)
4. 7 years
5. 17280 packets
6. £1.50
7. 5.64m
8. 73.10kg
9. Raheel = 199m and Adeel = 1.75m
10. Total £67200 Average £16800
11. 3600 words
12. 400 women
13. £450
14. £600
15. 36 sweets

Exercise 5

1. 7
2. 2
3. 16
4. 0
5. 10
6. 4
7. 6
8. 26
9. 6
10. 10

Exercise 6

1. 110
2. 96
3. 5
4. 26

Exercise 7

1. J
2. G
3. P
4. X
5. B
6. G
7. J
8. J
9. S
10. Y
11. T
12. F
13. U
14. V
15. C
16. 150
17. 156
18. 28
19. 75
20. 27

Exercise 8

1. D
2. A
3. D
4. B
5. E
6. E
7. C
8. D
9. D
10. A

Exercise 9

1.

$$\begin{array}{c} 35 \\ 63 \boxed{\div} 9 \\ 5 \end{array}$$

2.

$$\begin{array}{c} 18 \\ 12 \boxed{\times} 3 \\ 2 \end{array}$$

3.

$$\begin{array}{c} 72 \\ 62 \boxed{-} 26 \\ 36 \end{array}$$

4.

$$\begin{array}{c} 11 \\ 61 \boxed{-} 59 \\ 9 \end{array}$$

5.

$$\begin{array}{c} -7 \\ -22 \boxed{+} 36 \\ 21 \end{array}$$

6.

$$\begin{array}{c} 8 \\ 4 \boxed{\times} 16 \\ 8 \end{array}$$

7.

$$\begin{array}{c} 42 \\ 21 \boxed{+} 56 \\ 35 \end{array}$$

8.

$$\begin{array}{c} 121 \\ 22 \boxed{\div} 2 \\ 11 \end{array}$$

9.

$$\begin{array}{c} 0 \\ 12 \boxed{\times} 0 \\ 99 \end{array}$$

10.

$$\begin{array}{c} 6 \\ 16 \boxed{\times} 3 \\ 8 \end{array}$$

11.

$$\begin{array}{c} -10 \\ -5 \boxed{\times} 4 \\ 2 \end{array}$$

12.

$$\begin{array}{c} 93 \\ 153 \boxed{-} 111 \\ 51 \end{array}$$

Exercise 10

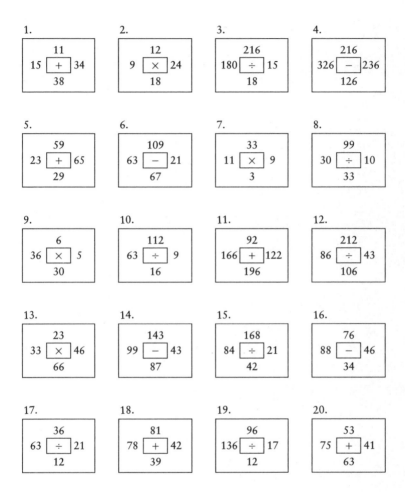

1.
	11	
15	+	34
	38	

2.
	12	
9	×	24
	18	

3.
	216	
180	÷	15
	18	

4.
	216	
326	−	236
	126	

5.
	59	
23	+	65
	29	

6.
	109	
63	−	21
	67	

7.
	33	
11	×	9
	3	

8.
	99	
30	÷	10
	33	

9.
	6	
36	×	5
	30	

10.
	112	
63	÷	9
	16	

11.
	92	
166	+	122
	196	

12.
	212	
86	÷	43
	106	

13.
	23	
33	×	46
	66	

14.
	143	
99	−	43
	87	

15.
	168	
84	÷	21
	42	

16.
	76	
88	−	46
	34	

17.
	36	
63	÷	21
	12	

18.
	81	
78	+	42
	39	

19.
	96	
136	÷	17
	12	

20.
	53	
75	+	41
	63	

Exercise 11
1. C   2. C   3. B   4. D   5. A   6. C   7. A   8. D   9. C 10. B
11. C 12. A 13. B 14. D 15. B 16. B 17. C 18. C 19. D 20. C

Exercise 12
1. C   2. B   3. C   4. D   5. B
6. C   7. D   8. A   9. D 10. C

2.   Flow diagrams (page 179)

Exercise 1

1.

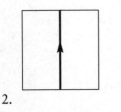

2.

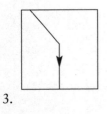

3.

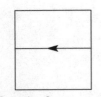

Exercise 2

1. court action
2. reminder sent
3. 60 days

Timed flow diagram exercise

1. letter of rejection sent
2. no further action
3. offer of post
4. applicant is invited to sit test
5. details of applicant are passed to management

3. Checking (page 185)

Exercise 1

Those company names with errors have been placed in brackets.

Original	*Copy*
Paine Chocolates	(Pain Chocolates)
Pall Mall Dispensing	Pall Mall Dispensing
Lodge Insurance Brokers	(Lodge Insurence Brokers)
Lodder Est Agts	(LOdder Est Agts)
Mill Hill Dry Clnrs	Mill Hill Dry Clnrs
Kahn Printers	Kahn Printers
Italian Piano Co	Italian Piano Co
Hoxtex Restaurants	(Hoxtex Restaurant)
Apollo Bed and Breakfast	(Apollo Bedand Breakfast)
Holloway Carpenters	Holloway Carpenters
Archway Halal Meat	(Archway Hala Meat)
Hookway Jewellers	Hookway Jewellers
Hi-tec School of Motoring	Hi-tec School of Motoring
Totland Hire Centre	(Totland Hire Center)
George's Recruitment	(Georges Recruitment)
West End Consultants	West End Consultants
Court Cars	(Court cars)
House of Lighting	(Hourse of Lighting)
Woxton Water Works	Woxton Water Works
Castletown Restaurants	(Castletown Recruitments)

Hardwood Doors Group Ltd	(Hardwood Doors Group LTD)
Mike's Do It Yourself Centre	Mike's Do It Yourself Centre
MITAKA Publishing House	(MITAKA Publsihing House)
Sunchung Takeaway	(Sanchung Takeaway)
Move Motorcycle Hire	(Move Motorcyycle Hire)
Portman Car and Van Rental	(Portman Carr and Van Rental)
Heitman and Son Accountants	(Heitman and son Accountance)
Ace Consulting Engineers	Ace Consulting Engineers
Hot Tandoori House	(Hot Tundoori House)
Safe Security Ltd	(Safe security Ltd)

Exercise 2

Original	*Copy*
ABC123	ABC123
ACCB/123/321	ACCB/123/321
CENTIMETRES/CUBIC	(CENTEMETRES/CUBIC)
GUMPTION	GUMPTION
MEASURES/CAPACITY	(MAESURES/CAPACITY)
987654321/123456789	987654321/123456789
987/123/654/456:	(987/123/654/456)
GERMANIUM-72.59	(GERMANUM-72.59)
MOLYBDENUM-95.94	MOLYBDENUM-95.94
NICKEL-58.71	(NICKLE-58.71)
ZIRCONIUM-91.22	ZIRCONIUM-91.22
PHOSPHORUS-30.9738	(PHOSPHOROS-30.9738)
MILLILITRES-36966	(MILLILITERS-36966)
MANGANESE-54.9380	MANGANESE-54.9380
DECAGRAMMES-15432	(DECAGRAMMS-15432)
KILOGRAMME-2205	(KILOGRAMMES-2205)
ANTIMONY-121.75	ANTIMONY-121.75
HYDROGEN-1.0080(H)	(HYDROGIN-1.0080(H))
CHROMIUM-51.996	(CHROMUIM-51.996)
MINNESOTA STATE	(MINNISOTA STATE)
ZEDEKIAH	ZEDEKIAH
WYOMING/CHEYENNE	(WYCOMING/CHEYENNE)
TENNESSEE/NASHVILLE	(TENESSEE/NASHVILLE)

ZOROASTER	ZOROASTER
PENNSYLVANIA/H'BURG	(PENNCYLVANIA/H'BURG)
WHISTLER	(WHISLER)
VERSAILLES	(VERSAILES)
VERRUCOSE	VERRUCOSE
UNHALLOWED	(UNIHALLOWED)
TREACHEROUS	TREACHEROUS
TREASURY	(TREASUERY)
SPARE-PART	(SPAIRE-PART)
ROUSSEAU	(RUOSSEAU)
EQUIVALENTS	(EQIUVALENTS)
FLOUNCE	(FLUONCE)
HARDENBERG	HARDENBERG

Exercise 3

Original   *Copy*

123/456/789/AC	123/456/789/AC
987/654/321/CA	987/654/321/CA
32323/452/CIC	(32332/452/CI(C)
ACEG/818/658	ACEG/818/658
BDFH/4653/12	(BDFH)4653/12)
ZED/678/TLT/010	ZED/678/TLT/010
WORLD/VIEW/83	(WORLD/VEIW/83)
ZEBEDEE/F/JJ	(ZEBFDEE/F/JJ)
YETI/SNOW/MAN	YETI/SNOW/MAN
ORI/GIN/AL/212	ORI/GIN/AL/212
ADVERTISEMENT	(ADVERITISEMENT)
PERSONNEL/DEPT	(PERSENNEL/DEPT)
COM/PUT/ER/SYS/TEM	(COM/PUT/ER/SyS/TEM)
00/11/22/345/678	00/11/22/345/678
3456/0987/4321/32	3456/0987/4321/32
RO/AD/RU/NN/ER/234	(RO/AD/RV/NN/ER/234)
GAL/2001/200001/00	(GAL/2001/20001/00)
ISBN 0–561–15163–0	ISBN 0–561–15163–0
1010101/02020/300	1010101/02020/300
DATA-100/303/404/50	(DATA/100/303/404/50)

4.   Coded instructions (2) (page 188)

1. [3]
2. [2]
3. [4]
4. [5]
5. [5]
6. [2]
7. [4]
8. [5]

5.   Coded instructions (3) (page 190)

1. [3]
2. [1]
3. [2]
4. [3]
5. [5]
6. [2]
7. [2]
8. [4]
9. [2]
10. [1]

6.   Sequencing (page 192)

A. 2, 6, 7, 3, 1, 5, 4
B. 2, 3, 1, 4
C. 4, 2, 1, 3
D. 5, 3, 4, 2, 6, 1
E. 2, 4, 3, 1
F. 3, 2, 1
G. 4, 2, 3, 1
H. C
I. Nephew and Aunt
J. S

Further reading from Kogan Page

Books

Career, Aptitude and Selection Tests: Match Your IQ, Personality and Abilities to Your Ideal Career, Jim Barrett, 1998

Great Answers to Tough Interview Questions: How to Get the Job You Want, 6th edition, Martin John Yate, 2005

How to Master Personality Questionnaires: The Essential Guide, Mark Parkinson, 1997

How to Master Psychometric Tests: Winning Strategy for Test-takers, 3rd edition, Mark Parkinson, 2004

How to Pass Computer Selection Tests, Sanjay Modha, 1994

How to Pass Graduate Psychometric Tests, 2nd edition, Mike Bryon, 2001

How to Pass Numeracy Tests, Harry Tolley and Ken Thomas, 1996

How to Pass Technical Selection Tests, 2nd edition, Mike Bryon and Sanjay Modha, 2005

How to Pass the Civil Service Qualifying Tests, 2nd edition, Mike Bryon, 2003

How to Pass the Firefighter Selection Process, Mike Bryon, 2004

How to Pass the New Police Selection System, 2nd edition, Harry Tolley, Billy Hodge and Catherine Tolley, 2004

How to Pass Verbal Reasoning Tests, Harry Tolley and Ken Thomas, 1996

Preparing Your Own CV: How to Improve Your Chances of Getting the Job You Want, 3rd edition, Rebecca Corfield, 2003

Readymade CVs: Sample CVs for Every Type of Job, 3rd edition, Lynn Williams, 2004

Readymade Job Search Letters: Every Type of Letter for Getting the Job You Want, 3rd edition, Lynn Williams, 2004

Successful Interview Skills, Rebecca Corfield, 1992

Test Your Own Aptitude, 3rd edition, Jim Barrett and Geoff Williams, 2003

CD ROMS

Psychometric Tests, The Times Testing Series, Editor Mike Bryon 2001

Test your Aptitude, The Times Testing Series, Editor Mike Bryon, 2001

Test your IQ, The Times Testing Series, Editor Mike Bryon, 2001

The above titles are available from all good bookshops. For further information contact the publisher at the address below:

Kogan Page Limited
120 Pentonville Road
London N1 9JN
United Kingdom
Tel: 020 7278 0433
Fax: 020 7837 6348
Website: www.kogan-page.co.uk

THE TIMES

Published by Kogan Page Interactive, The Times Testing Series is an exciting new range of interactive CD ROMs that will provide invaluable practice tests for job applicants and for those seeking a brain-stretching challenge.

Each CD ROM features:

- hundreds of unique interactive questions
- instant scoring with feedback and analysis
- hours of practice and fun
- questions devised by top UK MENSA puzzle editors and test experts
- against-the-clock, real test conditions
- a program that allows users to create their own tests

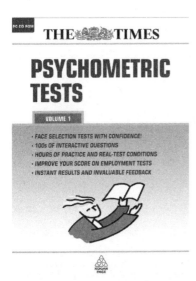

PC CD ROM
THE TIMES

PSYCHOMETRIC TESTS

VOLUME 1

- FACE SELECTION TESTS WITH CONFIDENCE!
- 100s OF INTERACTIVE QUESTIONS
- HOURS OF PRACTICE AND REAL-TEST CONDITIONS
- IMPROVE YOUR SCORE ON EMPLOYMENT TESTS
- INSTANT RESULTS AND INVALUABLE FEEDBACK

KOGAN PAGE

Psychometric Tests
Volume 1

Psychometric Tests Volume 1 provides essential practice for any job applicant who has to face a selection test.

With this CD ROM users will be able to:

- practise on tests based on those used by top employers
- learn how to tackle different types of questions
- experience real test conditions
- receive instant results and invaluable feedback

THE TIMES

Test Your IQ
Volume 1

This interactive CD ROM contains hundreds of questions just like those used in job selection IQ tests. *Test Your IQ* Volume 1 enables users to:

- practise for hours and achieve improved scores

- score against their friends

- develop their vocabulary and powers of logic

- practise on randomly selected tests every time

Test Your Aptitude
Volume 1

By working through the tests contained in this interactive CD ROM users will get a clear insight into what really makes them tick and the sort of job that would suit them best. *Test Your Aptitude* Volume 1 will reveal to users:

- what really motivates them

- which career best suits their personality

- their strengths and weaknesses

- how they will perform in selection tests